The Final Verdict

CH01424446

Christian greetings
Gillian Powe

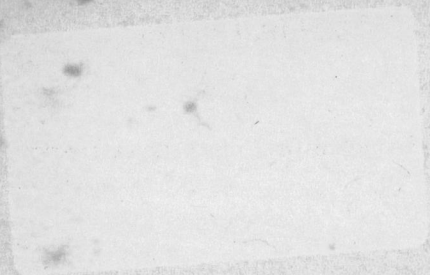

The Final Verdict

✳

The Sequel to *The Cross Between Thieves*

Gillian Powe

Marshall Pickering
An Imprint of HarperCollinsPublishers

Marshall Pickering is an Imprint of
HarperCollins*Religious*
Part of HarperCollins*Publishers*
77–85 Fulham Palace Road, London W6 8JB

First published in Great Britain
in 1997 by Marshall Pickering

1   3   5   7   9   10   8   6   4   2

A catalogue record for this book is
available from the British Library

ISBN 0 551 03124 7

Printed and bound in Great Britain by
Caledonian International Book Manufacturing Ltd, Glasgow

TO DAVID
MY HUSBAND AND VERY BEST FRIEND

✳

Contents

CHAPTER 1

✳

Mission Impossible?

Underestimating God's ability to break down barriers is not really a very good idea.

Lewes Prison Chapel was busy that lunchtime. The finishing touches were being made to the splendid painting behind the altar table, and paint, cloths and brushes were strewn haphazardly across the chapel floor. The prison orderly was tidying up as well as he could, but the air was heavy with the buzz of unfinished activity – and a distinct smell of paint.

Six visitors sat nervously at one side of the bright if chaotic room, trying to take in the nature of these unfamiliar and slightly frightening surroundings. Many months previously it had seemed a rather splendid idea to put their names down on a list. A simple action at the time, but one with far-reaching consequences for all of them. These five young men, in training to be Anglican vicars at Wycliffe Hall, Oxford, had volunteered to be part of a mission team to Lewes Prison in Sussex and, in spite of growing anxiety, they and their tutor had now arrived to begin seven days of practical evangelism experience.

Anyone who has been to college will know that confidence and a surfeit of conversation are hallmarks of the Common Room. However neither of these was present in the chapel that morning. In their place were nervous dispositions and the odd hesitant verbal exchange. Back in college, talk about evangelism, or telling people about Jesus, would have seemed serious but not really threatening. The students would have gone over possible responses that people might make when the subject of Christianity came up. Furthermore, each man would have been fairly sure of his own faith, not so that he would appear naïve or over confident but so that he was secure enough to inspire others and indeed to offer himself to the Church for full-time service. Now the crunch had come. The five were here in a prison setting preparing to walk out into those long and dreary wings to proclaim their message of hope to a rather difficult audience.

William was there, cultured, educated, a former barrister, matured by his own experiences of suffering and trauma. His confident speech and powerful faith would surely provide an ideal grounding for work in the prison, but his compassion and care for the inmates were to be the attributes my husband, David, the Chaplain, and I would most readily recall after his departure.

Chris was an open, friendly and street-wise student. We imagined he might have struggled to maintain his individuality in a college environment, but in the prison he was to be in his element. He had a keen heart for evangelism and a rejection of social taboos that might render a religious discussion inappropriate. He had an obvious desire to see a task through to the end and a real heart of gold.

Christopher was, on the surface, more self-assured. He was determined not to be flustered, was slow to worry and quick to pray. Through the week he rose to the occasion and had opportunity to reveal a sensitive heart and a care for the inmates.

Simon was the deep-thinking one who was aware of the spiritual battle raging on all sides. He felt driven to prayer for the situation and people at Lewes Prison. His quiet nature was a calming, reassuring influence when excitement was high.

Matthew was tall, dark and studious, and his nickname of 'Joe 90' suited him well. His calm exterior belied his enthusiasm and interest in the work with prisoners, and he was totally involved in the task set before him.

Philip came as tutor and leader of the group. A very well qualified Old Testament lecturer, but new to the college, he rose well to the very difficult task of being responsible for others in a situation also new to himself. His serious approach to the mission served both him and us well, and his concern not only for the men but for the nature of the mission itself was reassuring and affirming. He later wrote that the team had not so much come to run a mission but to take part in one that was taking place daily. Nevertheless, he and his team of young men did make a real mark on the chaplaincy, and we appreciated them greatly.

So this gifted but apprehensive group waited for David to issue their first instructions. Each clasped a neatly typed daily programme of events, enclosed in a new blue plastic wallet David and I had purchased hastily from W.H. Smith's the week before. Grouped in pairs, they were to be assigned to different members of the chaplaincy team to experience the breadth of activity that regularly took place in the prison.

Every prison has an Anglican chaplain by law, and although some vicars might feel that such a 'patch' might not be very strong ground for a meaningful ministry, David had found the exact opposite. With a simple message, even more simply expressed, he had gone to the cells of the prison offering men the opportunity to start again with God and begin a new life as Christians. Hundreds of men with a desire to meet God and change the course of their lives found new spiritual direction. You can read more of their stories in my book *The Cross Between Thieves*. It is unlikely that many of them would become instant middle-class, educated and totally responsible citizens, but change was very real and very obvious. Many gave up their drug-dependent existence, established more long-lasting relationships, studied the Bible, learned to pray and attempted to join up with Christian groups once they had left prison.

Each chaplain in one of Her Majesty's Prisons works in a team, with ministers from other denominations – Roman Catholic, Methodist, Salvation Army, etc. Other religions are represented by their spiritual leaders, and all operations are co-ordinated by the Anglican Chaplain. Outside visitors and Christians from various denominations often come in to assist the chaplain, and to meet prisoners in religious services and meetings. David had built his team up well, and volunteers came in daily to lead Bible study and prayer groups. As there were so many responding to the Christian message, there were always more inmates to follow up with support, teaching and advice.

It seemed good, too, to invite our ordinands, or 'trainee vicars' as they became known, to experience prison ministry, so that some might feel drawn to similar work, and all would broaden their understanding of working with such men as prisoners. Trainee vicars are no different from the rest of the community. They arrived with their preconceived ideas, prejudices and fears about the criminal world. Most people tend to class all those 'doing time' in the same category – men or women who are getting their just desserts, deserve no sympathy and are best forgotten. The reality is, of course, far more complex. The man incarcerated for nonpayment of his poll tax is banged up with the man steeped in crime, the income tax evader with the drug dealer. As in society at large, the prison populations are as varied as the communities they represent. Some prisoners seem to be quite frightening and even wicked, but others appear very unfortunate or even sociable and responsible.

Working in a prison with the hope of bringing people to God would seem to be a real 'mission impossible'. Are such people open to, or even worthy of, redemption? Society may respond, 'no' and of course, all of our inmates had been judged and rejected through their trials in courts of various kinds.

So each man had had to face the reality of his deeds, but maybe it is right to draw back and look at the whole picture for a moment. Just what is the case for the prosecution against these men in the moral sense? Are they the dregs of society worthy only of exclusion? Are we right to spend so much time working with these people? How strong is the case for leaving them to their own devices – for shutting them up and throwing away the key? Was it worthwhile bringing these students to experience ministry amongst such men? Consider some of our cases for a moment before you respond to these questions.

Many reasons for the rise in the crime figures are bandied about – poverty, decline of the nuclear family, poor education, job insecurity, and lack of morality are all cited and there is probably a little truth in all of them. However, time and time again we were to come across individuals who were inside not because they wanted to rob but because they needed to eke out yet another day's existence, supported by an ever-burgeoning drug habit.

Roy Kybett, one of our more longstanding and experienced volunteers, was helping a young man fill out a questionnaire from health care rehabilitation in order to place him in appropriate care after prison. Roy began to go down the list:

'Did you take drugs then, Mike?' he asked the young, almost waif-like boy in front of him.

'Oh yeah,' replied Mike readily, shrugging his shoulders a little and sniffing.

'Heroin?' questioned Roy.

'Yeah,' was the response. 'Three or four times a week.'

Roy carefully filled in the form.

'What about cocaine?' he queried.

'Oh yeah,' said Mike, 'I take that regular.' Then seeing a further clarification was expected, 'Well, most days really.'

Roy filled in the information.

As he carried on down the list Roy failed to find any substance not used regularly by Mike. Finally the ecstasy question seemed different.

'Well, no,' said Mike, 'not really. I only use that for special occasions – you know, parties an' that.'

Roy tried not to look fazed, and moved on to the alcohol section. There again Mike had a huge dependence, as he also proved to have on amphetamines and other pills. There was no area Roy could leave blank. Mike was just 19 years old. The expense of serving such habits can only be guessed at, but it's certain no 19-year-old could ever earn sufficient income to cover it all. Crime and plenty of it was the only alternative, and Mike had hundreds of offences both behind him and up for consideration this time. At least his attempt to enter 'rehabilitation clinic' was a move forward – perhaps a few less folk would wake to find their homes ransacked and their hard-earned possessions removed in order to fund a young boy's drug habits.

Joe was a fence. He acquired stolen goods from the likes of Mike and sold them on in pubs, clubs and at car-boot sales. He made his complete living this way, and was quite indignant at being caught and imprisoned. David tried to reason with this essentially likeable, easy-going chap when he began to talk about his family one day.

'You love your son, do you, Joe?' asked David.

'Sure,' replied Joe swiftly, 'I love him a lot.'

'Has he got anything in line for Christmas?' queried David.

'Sure, he's got a brand new mountain bike to come. It's the real biz.'

David smiled at Joe's happy face, and went on. 'Will he like it, then – this bike?'

'Course he will,' responded Joe vehemently. 'He'll be so proud, I know it.'

'Would he be sad if he woke up one morning and someone had nicked it?' asked David innocently.

'Sad? He'd be sad,' responded Joe swiftly, 'and I'd sure be mad if I found who nicked it – I'd kill him, I really would.'

David paused as he saw the enormity of the idea settling over Joe's previously jocular features.

'So do you think the parents of the boys whose bikes you fence would feel any less sad or mad then?' he questioned.

The nature of the sting crept slowly up on Joe, who coloured deeply and eventually replied, 'No, I guess they wouldn't. I've never thought of it at all like that.'

'Well, perhaps it's time you did,' said David, 'because I don't feel your son will grow up to be too proud of you if you carry on doing these things, do you?'

'No, I guess not,' responded Joe slowly.

David left him pondering this new thought about his life's activities. It would certainly take some time if he were to choose to change, and David assured him that he would certainly need God's help if he wanted things to be different.

Simon's career wasn't concerned with either drugs or fencing because he believed in the 'direct approach' to money procurement. He regularly committed armed robbery, with Securicor vans being his speciality. He was an older, well-built chap when David met him. Strong and tough-looking, he had dust-like hair and was no man with whom to argue. An Eastender, family was crucial to him, but, outside of his close knit circle, he was also a dangerous man.

He was suspected of robbery with extreme violence, as he had used a baseball bat to 'slow down' a couple of guards who chose to flee the scene of the crime. His apparent total disregard of the gravity of his crime was very obvious when he met David to request prayer for his sick daughter. He cheerfully explained his way of life, and boasted of his knowledge of the best places to set up a robbery.

'For example,' he volunteered, 'never do a job in Kingston.'

'Well, why not?' asked David, unable to resist the question in spite of its obviously dubious nature.

'Because there ain't no outers,' answered Simon. 'You can't get out of Kingston, you just go round and round the one-way system – it's not worth the hassle.'

When David later related this tale I could picture Kingston as well as he could. David had worked in a large store there before we met, and I had trained to teach in the town. I could well recall my father driving round and round the town centre, trying in vain to get into the necessary lane to leave for Kingston Hill. The shops seemed all too familiar the third time round!

The stories of these three men symbolize the nature of the lives of those with whom we work, and of course there are also those who have committed far worse crimes of all kinds. The case for the prosecution would appear to be rather strong. These men have contributed little to society, shown no degree of responsibility, and could well be labelled unworthy. Is this how we are going to think? If it is, then we fly in the face of the Bible. Make no mistake, many members of society do totally reject such men, and fiercely resent and resist attempts to rehabilitate or reform them. Even some Christians hold these views.

'They are bad people, you know,' David was told by a member of our local church. 'They deserve their time. Is there any real point in what you do?'

Another member of that church was an enthusiastic participator in the prayer line, but told me sadly, 'I'm so enthusiastic but I keep quiet about it here. Several people are not at all interested, they think it's a bit of a waste of time.'

The Bible, however, is full of hope for the worst and least in society. Nowhere will you read about the greater worthiness of the educated, rich and famous – quite the reverse is true. The pages are crammed with stories of those who found, or had been kept by, God, in spite of disobedience or crime.

Moses the great leader committed murder before leading the Jewish nation to the promised land. Samson's love of a woman nearly destroyed him, but he went on to a final act that demonstrated the power and authority of God. David stole Bathsheba, had her husband murdered, and spoilt his sons by self-indulgence, yet he is hailed as the greatest king and even as a forerunner of Christ himself. Saul was a wicked persecutor of Christians, causing many to be arrested, and standing by as Stephen was martyred. He went on to be the greatest evangelist the world has known. Matthew, a disciple of Christ, was a notorious tax collector, one of a group renowned for fraud and extortion, but he was a close friend of Jesus and the source of one of the gospel records. Indeed there is much precedent for regarding crime and immorality as no bar at all for a change of heart, and plenty of evidence that God shows no prejudice against bad men and women.

Jesus' teaching is full of directives not to judge others but rather to look at ourselves. For example, there is the story of the Pharisee and the tax collector, where pride in social position is deprecated, and we are warned not to value ourselves too highly. Jesus himself socialized with the disreputable and rejected, ate with tax collectors and sinners, and when a criminal crucified with him turned to Jesus he was assured of his forgiveness.

Our students from Oxford had to confront these issues that spring mission time. They knew the text of the New Testament, had even read it in the original Greek, and were well aware that Jesus' great and final commission was to go out into the world with the Gospel. They were also used to arguing the case for Christianity in response to the great issues of life, but here, in this cauldron of crime, despair and ignorance, all their knowledge and skills could swiftly prove to be irrelevant.

So it was some very nervous and awkward men who went on to the wings. Chris went with David down to the hospital area. On the way he talked about conversions and his worry about what to say to men such as these. He felt out of his depth. The hospital wing is long and thin, and lacks the normal busy atmosphere of an average hospital. Along with those who have broken limbs and other normal ailments, one finds those withdrawing from drugs, attempted suicide cases and the mentally unstable. Withdrawn from the rest of the prison, inmates are usually very pleased to see visitors of any kind, representatives of the chaplaincy being no exception.

'Well, what do we do now?' whispered Chris as he stood at the entrance with David, taking in the strangeness of the atmosphere and feeling rather ill at ease.

'Less of the we,' replied David. 'What are *you* going to do?'

Chris looked rather shocked. 'Me?'

'Yes, you,' responded David. 'Let's start with Barry over there.' With that he motioned towards the end of the ward where a huge inmate was standing, hands on hips, observing the two men who'd just come in. Barry, whose arms were heavily tattooed, made a striking picture in that doorway. Yet he had a twinkle in his eye as he bellowed down the corridor, 'Hey, come and convert *me*.'

Chris looked at David anxiously but got no reassurance there.

'He's talking to you,' said David. He had met Barry before and the big man obviously knew what was going on. Chris wasn't really being cast to the lions.

'You know his name,' David went on, 'so you can't ask that. Go and ask him if he'd like God to help him in his life. Go on.'

Something drove Chris to comply, but he wasn't sure what. He approached Barry hesitantly, and looking up at his towering frame he flustered, 'Well, hello there, Barry. I'm Chris. I'm working with the chaplain this week. Errm, have you thought ... I mean do you think ... I mean does God mean anything to you?' he finished lamely.

Barry looked mildly amused and suggested helpfully, 'You're supposed to ask me if I want God in my life.'

'Oh yes,' replied a very embarrassed Chris. 'Well, would you like God to help you in your life?'

'Yes,' was the firm reply. At this point Chris's mind went blank. He could think of no appropriate response. Instead he turned to David and mouthed, 'What do I do now?'

David approached the two men and suggested they all go into a side ward. He knew it was now time to take over.

An astonished Chris sat beside the large man as he explained his need for God to the chaplain. Within a few minutes David led Barry, like so many others before him, line by line, in a simple prayer. It went something like this:

'I am really sorry, God, for the life I've been leading. I'm really sorry. I can't cope any more. I want Jesus to come into my life and make a new start. Please help me. I really mean this. Amen.'

David laid his hands on Barry's head, prayed for him and asked God to fill him with his Holy Spirit.

Barry looked up slowly.

'My wife will be pleased, you know, she's been a Christian for years,' he smiled.

David asked Barry gently if he'd like to ring his wife and tell her the good news. 'Yes, I think so,' said Barry.

Getting an outside line, David rang Barry's wife and let the two speak.

'Hello, love,' said Barry, in a remarkably soft voice. 'I've been talking to the chaplain and I've become a Christian.'

There was a silence before a voice was heard saying 'I don't believe it!'

After a while, David took over, but he also had no real success in persuading her that her errant husband wished to change his ways. Obviously, even years of prayer had not prepared her for a positive answer to her requests. The change of circumstances was going to take a while to sink in!

Later, in the chapel, Chris admitted that he felt quite disoriented by the speed of Barry's change of heart. There had been no long-term counselling or discussion, but rather just a man in need of responding to the Gospel. The event challenged his whole expectation and training, but excited him too.

On another occasion William was with David, walking through 'B' wing looking for inmates to chat with. A very concerned officer approached David.

'They've got a ouija board in there, Chaplain,' the officer confided. 'I saw those things in the army, nothing but trouble, I don't like it.'

The man pointed nervously to one of the cell doors and looked for a response. David knew this officer had no faith of his own, but realized he obviously had a very healthy respect for the dangers of the occult. It was not uncommon for inmates to be involved in such practices – the prison librarian had admitted that she was often asked whether books on the subject were available.

'OK,' David responded. 'We'll go and check it out. Don't worry … and thanks for telling me.'

Later on that night William recalled the events of the morning. Sitting on the edge of his chair he told the others, 'It was over in three minutes – no, it wasn't – it was all over in two. I've never seen anything like it – it was incredible.'

He went on to describe the events as David had opened the door of the cell. Inside the cramped room four young offenders were sitting round the tiny table, concentrating hard. On the table they had carefully marked out a ouija board and, using a regulation mug, they were asking it questions.

The four were startled by David's abrupt entry, and all looked up. William stood behind him, possibly more surprised than the inmates themselves. David strode the two steps necessary to reach the table, picked it up and said firmly, 'Why are you doing this? This is very wrong. You are playing with fire, and who knows where it will lead? Would you let a child play with a nuclear bomb? Of course not – and neither will you play with this.'

He turned round and threw the offending object out of the cell door. By now the first officer had been joined by another, and they stepped back to avoid the table as it was propelled through the door.

'Throw it out and destroy it,' ordered David. No one argued. It was obvious he meant what he said. David turned back to the astonished men and declared, 'Don't you ever do that again. Now, we're going to pray.'

All four men looked down and began to comply, possibly out of astonishment.

'Hands together,' commanded David. 'Right, let's pray.'

He said a simple prayer asking God to forgive the men for playing with the ouija board, and casting out any wickedness that might have entered the room because of it. When he had finished he and the men looked up.

'Now,' he said, 'you all need God to help you. Would anyone like him now?'

One terrified man raised his hand, 'I would,' he said.

Ignoring the three others, two of whom had recovered enough to begin to snigger, the young man prayed with David, expressing a desire to become a Christian. Before he left, David told him to put his name down for chapel on the following Sunday.

'Oh yes,' he said quietly, 'I will.'

David and a shell-shocked William left the cell and returned to the chapel.

'Let him settle,' David told William, 'then go down and see him this afternoon with a Bible and tapes. Pray with him and we'll all pray for the others.'

After William had explained this astonishing event to his colleagues they all felt a burden for these young men who had chosen a ouija board to help them through prison. The students prayed earnestly. The prayer line was kept busy too.

The next day two of the others became Christians under the ministry of those students, and on the third day the final one decided that he too would like a better path for his life.

For him, James, this day turned out to be highly significant – firstly because he began a new Christian life on what was also his birthday, and secondly because he was 'shipped out' that evening to another prison, and we never saw him again. His name was passed on to Christians in his new prison, and we can only pray that what God started at Lewes, he would bring to completion.

All week the students prayed hard for and worked with the other three men, rejoicing to see them in chapel on the final day of the mission. William was especially thrilled to see them.

'I shall never forget it,' he confided in me. 'It was unbelievably thrilling. I really saw the power of God.'

That mission week 17 people became Christians, and the students were especially challenged and encouraged. They left with sadness on Sunday, after the service, and reported back enthusiastically and at length to fellow college members.

Chris went on to serve a curacy that had prison work involved, and William joined our prayer line to continue his commitment. All of them said they valued their experience, and felt it had affected their own ministry, especially in not underestimating the power of God in difficult lives, and in inspiring a boldness for the Gospel they had not felt before.

The experiences of these students have a relevance to our prosecution case against these criminals. Seemingly poles apart from the men they were serving, the students had found common ground in the love of God. These inmates were especially open and ready to receive Jesus compared to the trainee vicars' own non-believing contemporaries. Any prejudice just had to be laid to one side. God could work, and indeed was working, with such people. The case for the prosecution was just not that strong, as the chinks in its armour began to reveal. The finger of accusation could even be said to be turning round to face both them and us.

If these men were so obviously open to change and receiving the love of God, just why weren't there more of us in there telling them about him?

CHAPTER 2

✳

God's Bizarre Guest List

Jesus replied: 'A certain man was preparing a great banquet and invited many guests. At the time of the banquet he sent his servant to tell those who had been invited, "Come, for everything is now ready".'

But they all alike began to make excuses. The first said, 'I have just bought a field, and I must go and see it. Please excuse me.'

Another said, 'I have just bought five yoke of oxen, and I'm on my way to try them out. Please excuse me.'

Still another said, 'I have just got married, so I can't come.'

The servant came back and reported this to his master. Then the owner of the house became angry and ordered his servant, 'Go out quickly into the streets and alleys of the town and bring in the poor, the crippled, the blind and the lame.'

'Sire,' the servant said, 'what you ordered has been done, but there is still room.'

Then the master told his servant, 'Go out to the roads and country lanes and make them come in, so that my house will be full. I tell you, not one of those men who were invited will get a taste of my banquet.'

(Luke 14:16–24)

Speaking at churches, functions and organizations began to be a very regular event. Many people heard about the experiences at Lewes Prison, and David and I, together with various team members and Howard, an ex-prisoner, were pleased to share the news for two reasons. Firstly, we knew it was a great encouragement to Christians to hear of God working, and secondly, we were funding the purchase of literature.

It was obvious that people loved the stories of the individual men, but I was particularly determined to set the testimonies in a scriptural base. I began to be aware of certain passages that were especially relevant to our ministry, and would construct a format for a talk that would unify the passage and the work. David and I would work together on such a message, and then because we were talking to different groups all the time, were able to use it over and over again.

One of these passages was the parable of the great banquet in Luke, when Jesus tells of a man who was preparing a great banquet and who invited many guests. The invitations went out and notice of the date was given. When the great day dawned, messages were sent out to call the invited ones in, but instead of heading for the feast, one by one they made their excuses.

Jesus told stories that were set in his own time but which have meanings for all times. The man with the banquet is clearly God, who invites us all the join him in his Kingdom. Many today make their excuses as to why they won't join in too, just like the people in this passage.

The first said that he had bought a field and that he had to pay it all his present attention, so obviously he couldn't come to the banquet. How like today; many of us have possessions ludicrously beyond our needs, and looking after them is a huge job. How could we spare time to worship, and meet Christians, and even think about God when the car needs cleaning, the house needs painting, and the caravan and boat need getting ready?

The second man said he had just bought five yoke of oxen and would have to see they were set to work. He had a real job to do and he couldn't possibly spend time out now – maybe later! Similarly today many have demanding or interesting jobs that take up so much time they can think of little else. Unfortunately, people are valued in our society simply by virtue of the job they hold. 'He's a teacher,' we say, 'or a doctor or a company director. She's an engineer, an MP or a solicitor.'

For those left outside this world of work there is only disenfranchisement, low esteem and even despair but yes, the man in the story lives in our society too.

A third man claimed he had just got married so he couldn't be expected to think about God. He had his relationship and a new life to build. Well, we all know how much time and effort we put into relationships – they can be a great distraction. We may choose not to attend the feast on these grounds too.

Back at his master's house the servant messenger reports, and what is the response? 'Go back and persuade them'? 'Tell them I need them'? 'These are the people I want'? Well, actually no. The response turns out to be quite different. The master is angry – these people were clearly invited and have chosen not to come. Now the servant must go into the streets and alleys, and bring in the poor, the crippled and the lame.

Never mind the well-to-do, invite in the ones everyone else has forgotten: those with no money to buy possessions, those who do not have high-flying jobs, those without any supporting relationships.

What a message for today! As we went round churches together, David and I often saw people putting hours and hours into trying to persuade their friends and peers to find God and become Christians. We all want our nearest and dearest to come to God, and must go on trying, but the message of this passage is clear, even if in some cases unwelcome. Go and offer the Good News to others. Bring in the rejected, the poor and the sick. Make sure you tell them about the Gospel too. Furthermore the story goes on, because there is yet more room at the banquet. So the servant is sent out again, this time to the roads and country lanes so that there would be a full house for the feast.

So we too must go further from home, into the most undesirable places, where we least expect to find candidates for Christianity, in order to fulfil God's command to bring everyone in. Perhaps if we dare we may even have to enter prisons, to see if there are any there who would like to come to the feast. Of course the amazing thing, in both this story and today, is that all these unexpected people did come. They weren't full of excuses about whether or not they could fit in the occasion. We are only given the impression that they took their places with gratitude.

Talking about the passage often struck home forcefully with audiences and they would begin to own up to their own prejudices and presuppositions. It did seem that God was choosing a very different guest list than ours for his table.

Mick was an almost wild character whom Roy Kybett met in the hospital wing. He obviously suffered from some mental problems, and was being helped by the doctors and psychiatrists. He was a man of immense stature and long, unkempt dark hair. Roy and David both knew that Mick had as much right to be offered Jesus as any other inmate, and David duly paid him a visit one afternoon. His response was as surprising as it was immediate: he needed help in his life and was not afraid to admit it.

Later that week Roy went in search of Mick to help him with a Bible study. He knew this was going to be difficult, and he just had to trust that Mick would be calm and receptive. Mick was not on the hospital wing when Roy called, but was reported to be in education 'doing pottery'.

Roy made his way to the education department, wondering if his help was going to prove worthwhile. On arrival he looked round the room, glancing at all the inmates attending studiously to their pieces of clay. There was no sign of Mick's wild and woolly hair and his huge frame.

Roy approached an officer and asked for Mick. 'Oh yes,' he replied, 'he's over there,' and pointed to the centre of the room. There was Mick sitting at a potter's wheel working hard to comply with whatever instructions he had received. Roy was startled. Was this really Mick? Roy was momentarily thrown as he realized that Mick had cut off virtually all his hair, leaving only the merest covering, commonly called a 'dust cut'.

As Roy approached he saw that Mick was dealing with his clay in a rather aggressive fashion, lifting it up and pounding it on to the surface of the turntable, making the whole structure jolt under the strain. Mick's concentration was total, and although his demeanour was somewhat threatening, Roy knew that the object of the aggression was indeed the clay.

Gulping hard, Roy set out to make some sense of his mission. Obviously the Bible study was out, but Roy wanted Mick to know he had had a Christian visitor that day.

'OK, mate?' ventured Roy nervously, standing by Mick's side as the pummelling of the clay continued.

'Umph,' was the only reply, but Roy took it as an affirmative response, and went on, 'Well, that looks good, Mick. What are you making?'

Roy waited. A full minute later Mick replied, 'I'm making a dish, a clay dish,' and carried on battering his potter's wheel.

'Well, that's nice,' said Roy. 'I can see now it's a pot.' Roy was struggling, and realized that this conversation was not going to be of a sustained and meaningful nature. He made one more attempt. 'Who's it for then, Mick?' he asked, with as positive a tone as he could muster.

There was a further silence, but Roy could see that Mick was planning his reply.

Finally the huge man said, 'I'm making it ... for you,' and with that he stopped thumping and turned round to face Roy. '... for helping me,' he concluded, and resuming his potter's task he turned away once more.

'Thanks, Mick, thanks very much, mate,' stammered Roy before threading his way back through the class to the door. Once outside he started to allow himself to think about what had happened. He was concerned about Mick, and somewhat threatened by him too, but there was no doubt this man had made a glimmer of response to God. He'd tried to tidy up his appearance and was making Roy a clay pot. Only God can gauge the significance of such actions, but I would dare to guess they are of equal value with some of the noblest efforts some of us have made, we who have had every advantage over Mick in so many other ways. Just as I was thrilled with my own son's genuine first gift to me, so God is pleased with the tiniest step in the life of a man such as Mick. God had asked Mick to the banquet and he had responded.

Brian was an altogether different character. He was an astute and street-wise contract killer, who would deal with or 'sort out' problem people. When David met him he was working as a cleaner on the segregation wing. This is the part of the prison put aside for those who have broken prison rules and are too dangerous to be on the ordinary wings. A squat, stocky man, he had a short haircut and a very creased face. 'Like a creased ironing board,' another inmate once commented.

Brian had no front teeth as they had been knocked out during various fights. His reputation ensured that he was feared and respected on even the segregation wing, and his inability to either read or write was no bar to his holding the highest position. He had taken part in incidents involving razor blades in toothbrushes, and in knee-cappings using a baseball bat, selected for its lightness and ease of swing. So it was no wonder really that most inmates gave him a wide berth.

Nevertheless, David felt he was to be offered the Gospel just like everyone else, and so when he got the opportunity he took it. 'Would you like God to help you, Brian?' asked David cautiously one day.

David was used to people turning the offer down as well as accepting it, but he had also grown to realize that trying to guess a man's response was an empty task, so it wasn't a real shock when Brian replied, 'I could do with some help right now.'

Brian went on to repent of his past and to find Jesus as a new friend. David asked, 'Why have you decided to do this today, Brian?'

'Well,' replied Brian thoughtfully, 'I never thought about it before. Well, not for me, anyway. My sister's a Christian, I think. She lives abroad. But I didn't realize it was for blokes like me. I'd like a new start.'

In the weeks that followed Brian was a regular chapel-goer, and attended Roy's Bible studies in his corridor. He told David he felt better and that the Bible studies helped him.

'But you can't read, Brian, can you?' David gently questioned.

'No,' replied Brian, 'I can't, but I listen to learn, and talk of course. You know something?'

'What's that?' asked David.

'I hold this Bible in my pocket,' said Brian, pulling out his small brown New Testament, donated by the Gideons and given to him on his first day as a Christian.

'When I'm tempted,' Brian continued, 'I put my hand in my pocket and I feel God's Word right there. I feel the pages and I think of God's love going right through me.'

In the early days of Brian's conversion, officers kept asking him what he had in his slightly bulging pocket, because of course they always had to look out for any trouble, but after a while they remembered that Brian always carried his New Testament around and stopped asking him.

One day he asked to see David, who found Brian was beaming with pleasure.

'I wanted to tell you how I'm getting better,' Brian declared. David sat and waited for the tale to unfold.

'Well,' said Brian, 'there's this little tyke who fell out with me over some burn. [A prison term for tobacco.] Well, he wound me up, and in the end he wrote a note saying he hopes my mother dies of cancer.' Brian paused and David winced. Both knew Brian's mother had succumbed to that dreadful disease only months before, and although the man could not have known this it made the appalling insult worse. Brian continued his story.

'Well, of course I wanted to sort the bloke out – no one says that and lives.' David sat up and took careful note of this suggestion.

'Well then, I did something incredible,' pronounced Brian, this time pausing for effect and hoping for a response.

'What was that then?' questioned David.

'I warned him,' said Brian, triumphantly. 'I *really* warned him,' his voice hit a high note of satisfaction before dropping lower to add, 'I've never done that before, never, not just warned someone! So I guess I'm getting better.' Brian sat back and waited for an acknowledgement.

'Well, that's very good,' said David, shaking his hand firmly. 'Well done, Brian, that's a real step forward'.

David just couldn't wait to recount this story to us all, and found it hard not to grin, although he knew that this really did represent a step forward for a man such as Brian.

That afternoon Brian went on to ask for help. He had a brother whom he hadn't seen for some time, and Brian wanted him to visit him. He needed someone to contact his brother. So it was that Roy found himself driving up to a rubbish tip, seeking out a man who worked there, who was related to Brian. Roy alighted from his car and approached a couple of men emerging from a caravan in order to shunt piles of junk from place to place.

'I'm looking for Jim,' said Roy, as he approached the two men.

'Who's looking for him?' was the reply.

'Well, I'm a friend of his brother's, and I've got a message for him,' replied Roy, feeling uneasy.

'Who are you then?' One of the sturdily built men stepped towards Roy.

Now Roy was no wimp. An ex-heavyweight wrestler, he was often mistaken for an ex-inmate himself, and he would even joke about being out on licence now and then. Nevertheless he could spot danger when he saw it, because he knew Brian was inside for an unpleasant incident concerning baseball bats and a certain local rubbish tip. He took a step back and, taking a deep breath, he declared, 'I'm a member of the chaplaincy team at Lewes Prison, and Brian asked me to get a message to his brother to see if he'll visit him!'

He finished and looked up at the men. He never knew what had eased the situation; it could have been the message itself, the unlikely nature of this religious man, or even just his tone of earnestness, but whatever it was, it worked. The men looked hard at Roy and one said, 'We'll pass the message on.'

Roy knew when he'd outstayed his welcome, turned swiftly round and paced quickly back to his van.

Three days later the larger of the men turned up to visit Brian, who was very grateful to Roy. Although he was not half as relieved as Roy that the incident was over.

Brian grew as a Christian, and on his release linked up with another Christian in Birmingham for help. He wanted to make a new start far from his old haunts. With determination like that who's to say he won't succeed? We certainly pray that he does.

Would you say Brian was an odd selection for the royal banquet? If you did I would have to agree, but fortunately it's not you or I who draw up the guest list!

So I could move on to tell you of other men whom God was to draw near to himself in Lewes Prison, all of whose lives make untidy and in some cases disturbing reading. Why did God call Jake to be a disciple in prison, for example? He was accused of a multi-million pound fraud, and had travelled the hotels in Britain using false names – a real con man if ever there was one!

And why was Ted chosen? He planned the armed robbery of an off-licence, dressing up in combat jacket, army boots and balaclava. He made a plan of the area and timed the offence carefully – except that, forgetting that Wednesday was half-closing, he got caught outside the shop.

Dave tried to rob a fish and chip shop of its charity takings, needing the cash for drugs. However, the owner had glued the box to the counter, and rendered Dave near senseless with a huge piece of cod he had been battering. Staggering outside Dave and his friend were caught because they drove the wrong way down a one-way street and crashed their vehicle.

André found faith too. Very quiet and composed, he kept himself to himself and would sit listening to tapes and reading his Bible in his cell. One evening a group of five men pushed their way in at 'association time', because they were after the simple gold chain he always wore round his neck.

It was only then we discovered the truth about André. He wedged the door behind them and broke the first four men's noses in the ensuing fight. Then he calmly opened the door and threw the last man over the landing rail on to the safety nets below. He then turned to an officer and quietly reported the incident. It turned out he had been a trainer in the South African equivalent to the SAS – not a man with whom to trifle.

Later André was moved to the Isle of Wight, where he was followed up by our Korean volunteer, Bruce, who enjoyed fellowship with him and tried to ensure that André was set up on a good future path.

Ted was an abused child who turned abuser. Married to a woman with two children from a previous relationship, he abused them and her until she finally turned him in. High on drugs, he assaulted and committed acts of indecency against her. Yet he found God in his prison cell. Could this be possible?

Can men such as Ted and André, Dave or Jake, find God? Can the Brians and Micks be part of God's great planned banquet? The simple answer is

Yes. The power of God is not limited by our understanding, neither is his favour extended only to 'nice' people. The Gospel has the power to offer a new start to everyone, including people such as these examples from prison. These men are sincerely invited to God's feast even if the final guest list strikes us as totally bizarre.

CHAPTER 3

✳

A Day in Court

Howard had been our orderly at Lewes for many months, and he had taken his job very seriously. Quite apart from cleaning up the chapel and serving at the various services, he had brought many men to the chapel and helped them on the wings when they became Christians.

When his story came out in *The Cross Between Thieves* he was thrilled to read about his life and the change of lifestyle that took place in prison. He had, however, one reservation. 'It's all so out of date,' he said when he had finished the book. 'So much more needs to be said.'

Since his time in Lewes he had been dramatically moved to the Isle of Wight, and had his Christian commitment thoroughly tested by a tighter regime and by other Christians who doubted the reality of his faith. But he pulled through, obtaining an earlier parole than expected, taking up opportunities to tell churches and other groups about his new faith and trying to encourage support for the work inside Lewes Prison.

Howard once explained to me how it felt when you are sent for trial at court. 'Once you get in that van,' he said gravely, 'your life is out of your own hands. It's all up to other people now. You feel so powerless. There's nothing you can do about it.' It is interesting that he centred round the idea of powerlessness. Many prisoners are used to feeling in control because their crimes make others afraid of them and give them an illusion of self-esteem. Coming into prison is a huge shock, giving them a more realistic new perception of their status in the eyes of society.

Joe picked up the idea later that week, as he chatted to David.

'The judge is everything,' he claimed. 'If he gets to know you it can mean trouble. If I do something in Judge X's area I'll move to London and get caught for something there. Then the local charge is brought up to the London court and dealt with. It can save years off a sentence. Believe me: I know.'

Especially difficult, I've been told, is the lot of vulnerable prisoners whose turn comes to go to court. Due to the risk of other inmates attacking them because of the nature of their crime, they have to be protected as they go in and out of the common parts of the prison. One man from the protected 'K' wing, called Shane, shared with me his experiences of attending court.

7.00 a.m.   **Bang. Bang. Bang!** 'Jones, come on Jones, time to get up for court. What did you say? Talk like that and you're nicked boy!'

My pad [cell] mate tells me to push off as I've woken him up with a brew [cup of tea]. Ungrateful bloke!

7.15 a.m. I've washed, cleaned my teeth and dressed, and I'm ready to go to Lewes Crown Court. I know I'm going to prison 'cos otherwise I wouldn't be in front of 'Send 'm down Brown'.

7.30 a.m. Door opens. Two screws stand there. As a protected prisoner I need a guard.

7.35 a.m. A brisk walk out of the block to Reception. Loads of people milling about changing from prison clothes to their own (they're going to court, to a hospital – or they're going home).

7.40 a.m. The changing rooms are clear. The two screws guard me. No one speaks to me, just knowing looks all round.

7.50 a.m. I'm searched and ready to go into the box. That's a room with a bench for the Rule 43 prisoners [those named '43' are given extra protection under the 43rd rule of the prison system].
'Do you want breakfast, Jones?'
'No,' I reply, and have a fag.
The time drags slowly by.

9.30 a.m. The long wait is over. The door opens and I'm ready to go. One last search – no cuffs as I'm in the sweat box [prison vehicle]. I get into the van. They put me in a cube [term used to describe each section in the prison van] so you have to sit.

9.40 a.m.   The engine roars into life and we go for our ten-minute drive to the crown court. I've waited two hours for this. We could have walked in twos, just like school, but they have to waste a grand of tax payers' money.

9.50 a.m.   So we get to Lewes Crown Court and they off-load us. The other prisoners into a large holding room and me into a Beast Box [tiny, separate room for segregated prisoners, often known as 'beasts' due to the nature of their crimes].

9.55 a.m.   Then you get a brew and settle down to wait for your barrister to come. In the meantime you read the walls and find out how much of a slag your bird is, 'cos you find out she's been having sex with what seems like half the prison. Then you write on the walls too. The door opens and some bloke who looks about 19 says, 'Mr Jones, your barrister's here. Come this way please'.

In the old days the screws took you. It was just, 'Jones, your barrister's here.' Now it's Mr this and Mr that. It's a joke. We mess them about and there's nothing they can do. I plod along to see my barrister and pass the holding room. An inmate sees me and shouts, 'Jones, you've had it, bacon.' [This term of abuse is derived from bacon bonce = nonce, and is used to threaten unliked prisoners.]

'I'm gonna kill you,' shouts the man.

Then everyone is at their door joining in with their pound's worth. They kick the doors and shout abuse about my bird and my mother, and the bloke from the security company is scared stiff.

I'm in the interview room and a guard stands at the door, although as it's glass, they can all still see me. My solicitor and the barrister await me. My solicitor asks me, 'How's it going?'

I answer 'Great,' but not meaning it of course, because I can still hear them yelling 'beast' through the door.

10.00 a.m. The barrister tells me what is going to happen today. 'Right, today it's pleas and direction. You are going guilty on the handling and the theft and not guilty on the burglary.'

Of course I'm not asked my opinion during all this. 'You will get JR'd [Judge's remand].' I argue with him. I want to keep my present remand status. I stand my ground because I know how it works. My solicitor pays this barrister and I kinda pay him, so he's sacked if he doesn't pay attention to my instructions. The two professionals have a bit of a row and my solicitor wins.

10.30 a.m. We are going to court at 3.30 p.m., I'm told. So as it's only 10.30 a.m. I have to trek back to my box and wait. I sit here alone with nothing to do.

12.30 p.m. They bring my dinner. It's microwaved rubbish.

3.25 p.m. I ring my bell. The guard comes. I am desperate for the toilet. They don't want me to go as I'll be late in court.

3.40 p.m. I arrive late in court and my barrister shakes his head. The judge enters. 'All stand,' says the clerk.

I look at this man who can take my freedom away, and watch him smile at me. The judge doesn't appreciate me pleading not guilty when I'll obviously plead guilty at the end of the day. I don't respond.

3.50 p.m. It's nearly over. I plead not guilty anyway and I'm put on the list for two months' time.

'Take Jones down,' says the judge.

3.55 p.m. I'm back in my box.

4.05 p.m. My guard comes to get me.

'Is my barrister here?' I ask, eager to find out what's going on next.

'No,' replies the guard. 'You're going back to prison all by yourself.' With that the cuffs are on and I'm placed in a Ford Fiesta and driven back to prison. I'm cuffed to a bird who works for the security firm. She rambles on about my nearly causing a riot back there. I swear quite a bit at her.

4.15 p.m. I arrive at reception and for some reason I'm sent straight down the block to a strip cell. The search includes me having to squat. I'm told to dress.

4.45 p.m.   I get back into my cell with a cig and a
brew. I tell my cell mate my day's been a
total waste of space. I get little sympathy
but it made me feel just a little bit better.

Time after time this idea of powerlessness in court
is mentioned. The judicial system is a world apart
from most of us, with its own language and code of
practice. The uneducated or unable often respond
by using language and behaviour which only
serves to bring even more trouble on their heads.
They often simply don't have the language either to
explain their feelings or articulate their needs and
questions. However, they all have one thing in
common – they will tell you all about it. In prison
someone who listens is a very rare person indeed.

Most of our prisoners were on remand or waiting for a decision about their future. If found innocent they never returned to us but were released
into the community, but if declared guilty they
knew they would not only be returned to prison
but more than likely be sent on to a new establishment. We often witnessed that tension the day
before a final court appearance, and knew that they
felt quite unable to think beyond that next day. We
always offered prayer on such occasions if we were
aware of the event, and asked God for justice to be
done in that court room. We could often only ask
for this, as frequently we did not know the facts of
the case in hand.

The men usually felt content with this approach.
Sometimes we felt it right to pray only for mercy,
since no other plea was appropriate, and occasionally

we made a strange and individual request. Andy was such a case. He was due in court to face burglary charges. He had been interested in Christianity for some time, and one day came to chapel where he found a true and living faith. To say his appearance was unusual was an understatement. Standing six foot two in height, he was a large, imposing figure whose hair was bundled up behind his head in a huge lump. He told us that when let down it reached his legs. However, his hair was almost unnoticeable compared to his general appearance. There was no need to ask him his profession – he was a tattooist who had practised his art almost exclusively, it would seem, on himself. There was barely an inch of his limbs not covered with skilful tattooing. He was the sort of character you just couldn't help staring at, and the fascination of seeing tattoos on eyelids, ears and well into the hair line could not easily be ignored.

Andy knew this, of course, and actually was neither cross nor anxious about being the object of such attention. Nevertheless, on this Sunday morning he was worried.

'I'm a Christian now,' he said. 'I know I've done wrong, I admit it. I've made a new start but I know I must pay.'

'That's good,' said David, 'you're doing fine.'

'Yes, I know,' said Andy, twisting his hands together anxiously, 'but I know what everyone thinks, I don't think anyone will believe me. They'll think I'm all bad because of this.' Here Andy indicated his tattoos, pointing at his face, and sweeping his hands across his brightly coloured arms. 'What can I do? What can God do?'

'Let's pray,' suggested David, uncertain of what to say, but trusting that the words would be forth-coming.

Andy gratefully sat in an attitude of prayer, obviously waiting for help, and David looked at this trusting figure who just wanted a fair deal. And, from somewhere, the words came.

'O God,' he prayed, 'we ask for mercy for Andy. Please may he appear quite white when he's in court. May the people in that court just see his orig-inal features and colour.'

David continued to pray for a few minutes more, and then the two sat up and looked at one another.

'Is that possible?' asked Andy.

'I guess it is,' replied David. 'Our God can do anything.'

Andy seemed satisfied and left the chapel that morning, telling us his case was on Friday and that he'd see us next Sunday before he was shipped out, and let us know what happened.

We never did see Andy again. The next Sunday no tattooed face appeared at the chapel entrance. We could only guess at what had happened. We just prayed that all had been well and that God had helped Andy out in the way we had all hoped.

Two months later David told this story in a church in Burgess Hill. At the end of the service a woman virtually ran up to David as he packed his books and papers into his small black briefcase.

'Excuse me, I'm a probation officer. I was there,' she blurted out. 'I saw Andy – we all saw Andy in court that day.' Here she grew quite excited. 'He just looked normal! No one noticed anything. The judge was remarkably lenient. He seemed to take to Andy and believed he was sorry and had made a new start. He got sent to a probation hostel in the north.

'It was only after it was all over we noticed his face. I couldn't believe it. How could I have missed those tattoos? He looked so – well, strange. If I'd noticed I wouldn't have been able to see anything else. How did I miss them?'

She looked at David, waiting for a confirmation of what she had already guessed.

'It was the power of prayer,' stated David, quietly wondering to himself at the amazing result of that prayer. How good it was too that God had allowed us to know what had happened!

The story ended satisfactorily for Andy, and he was relieved to be given what amounted to a second chance. For many, of course, the story is different, not only because they end up imprisoned, but because they feel let down, confused and exhausted by the whole procedure.

For instance, I talked to Dan, sent down for his part in a very unpleasant fight which ended in a tragic death.

'You cannot bear the suspense in the end. It goes on and on and you get more and more confused about it all. You can't wait just to know,' he said.

Inmate after inmate confided the same information. The tension and sheer length of time before the resolution of a case caused the worst stress. Many of us will know that the cases we witness coming to a close on television refer back to incidents many months, sometimes even years, before.

These gaps have to be borne by everyone involved in the case and can seem interminable.

Jack told me he found all the evidence upsetting because he could not answer when the things being said weren't true, but this distress paled against the awful waiting, the not knowing.

Once convicted many are able to come to terms with even long stretches – at least then they know the result and can mentally prepare for the future.

Perhaps it was this powerlessness and the period of tense uncertainty about which we have spoken, that rendered so many men ready to respond to the offer of help and purpose that comes from God. Some might argue that only those who find God in a careful, reasoned way during a stable time have made a genuine decision to become a Christian. I do not believe the gospels record this, or that it can be universally applied today either. For many it is a point of crisis, deep searching or uncertainty that wakes us from our apathy or indifference and causes us to face spiritual truths. A few may approach God out of pure intellectual desire, but most of us recognize our own sin, inadequacy and need, and turn as a child does to its parent, hardly knowing what changes will be ahead once we have dared to allow God to enter our lives.

Whatever the theory, our evidence was clear: man after man chose to follow God before or during their time in court, and we certainly rejoiced that they were not alone, either in the dock or later in their cells once sentenced. Of course, any decision was only the beginning, and the journey of faith would be long and hard for many – but every-one has to start somewhere!

Sometimes people would question the men's change of heart, and insist that Jesus called us to be made disciples, not just converts, as if men could become disciples without first choosing to follow Jesus Christ. Our reading of the Bible is that faith as small as the tiny mustard seed is acceptable to God, and it is a concept we hang on to, both in prayer and action.

Of course the experience of court is threatening and distressing to all – victims, witnesses and rela-tives alike – and the defendants are usually the only people who can be said to deserve to be there.

Few of us will stand accused in a court room, and we can be thankful to God for that, but however strange it may seem, this awesome experi-ence has been used by God to bring people to himself, and for that we can be very grateful too.

CHAPTER 4

✳

Angels in My Peter

In court, prisoners are aware of the authorities that hold sway over their lives. They are not islands on their own doing as they please, but are answerable to other people and organizations. However, these earthly institutions are not the only elements to assert power over their, and indeed over our, lives. Even in this highly materialistic and earthly-centred society we are aware of a degree of 'other' worldliness. For most people their busy and relatively stable lives often crowd out spiritual things, and they might even be led to regard them as meaningless or at least irrelevant. However, prison, possibly like other crisis situations, has a remarkable power to concentrate the mind on the true nature of reality.

Unfortunately, probably due to a lack of Christian witness and example in their lives, prison inmates are drawn to the darker side of the spiritual world. As the incident with the ouija board in chapter one illustrated, there were plenty of opportunities to look into the unpleasant side of life. David routinely asked inmates whether they had had any

45

dealings with the occult, although he didn't use that term, as it was often not understood. Laurence was one such new Christian to whom David posed that question.

'Have you had dealings with ouija boards, Laurence?' asked David. 'If you have, we'll need to pray it through and out, so that God can change you fully.'

'No,' replied Laurence confidently, 'I haven't touched a ouija board at all.' He shook his head vigorously and then screwed up his eyes, obviously thinking hard.

'I've done satanism in graveyards,' he added, 'does that count?' David paused, looked at him straight in the eyes, and said quietly but firmly, 'Yes, it does count, Laurence, it really does count. I think we'd better pray over this one right now.'

Another lad called Jason became a Christian the same month. He was a sad, lonely person who had become involved in drugs and crime at an early age.

'I want a new start,' he declared, 'I really do.' As David was praying with him moments later, he felt he should ask Jason a question. 'Do you have a pain in your neck, Jason?' he asked, 'and somewhere else?' He paused, 'But I don't know where.'

This word of knowledge had slipped into David's head and he knew he had to ask Jason. The young man started and sat upright.

'How did you know?' he asked David. 'I do have a pain there, and I've got a pain in my big toe – just there,' he added, bending down to indicate which toe was hurting.

Jason had denied involvement in strange practices prior to praying with David, and the source of the pain was unknown. David tried once more because he had learned that persistent inexplicable pains were often linked to evil events.

'Are you sure you've had no links with ouija boards, Jason?' he asked carefully, and then, 'or your family? Is anyone in your family linked to these things?'

Jason looked straight at David and light seemed to dawn. 'Oh yes,' he replied, 'I've not done anything, but my sister's a witch, she used to say things over me all the time. She's been doing that for years.'

The innocent look on his face made David resolve to explore more broadly in future. Jason was being straight – after all, he'd been asked if he had ever been involved in occult practices and *he* hadn't, but his sister ... well, that was a different question altogether.

These simple stories reveal the astonishing vulnerability of people to become involved in evil without realizing it. Perhaps it also explains why some of them were so responsive to the Gospel. The idea of the other-worldly, the inexplicable, being possible was not totally alien to their experience. For them the world was not restricted to a rational series of events, all of which result from simple cause and effect. Yes, they were used to controlling their own destiny on the streets and resented the authority of the law and state infringing on their activities – but strange events and the power of the paranormal, that did not really surprise or horrify them as it generally would more law-abiding members of society.

Jason's pain left him after prayer, and he was relieved. Now he was to start a new life no longer controlled by such evil forces, and only the presence and power of the Holy Spirit would keep him safe in future. Without God's help we are all open to strange forces, however materialistic we may consider ourselves to be. The presence of God in our lives is the only means by which we can be sure that we are safe from evil influence. This may not be modern thinking but it is certainly Christian thinking, and we have witnessed the reality of it.

However, although we are aware of a significant amount of involvement in the occult in the prison, there was activity of a more wholesome kind too. Some of the events could be dismissed by a sceptic as wishful thinking, but we believe that God was working in that place, and that the 'coincidences' and remarkable events were too frequent and persuasive to be dismissed lightly.

Doug was a mature, quiet man whose arrival at the prison had thrown him into utter turmoil because he was charged with offences of a sexual nature. He was placed in the special part of the segregation unit set aside for vulnerable prisoners. Here, any who needed segregating for their own protection would spend their term, hoping never to be the victim of the other prisoners' surprising hatred for those who had committed what, in their eyes, were unacceptable crimes.

Doug was unlucky. Someone had read about his alleged activities and was quick to establish his presence on that wing in Lewes Prison. The segregation unit is set in a low position in the establishment, close to the inmates of 'F' wing. These convicted prisoners are often older and more settled than other inmates, and in this case a group planned their own scheme for retribution. Doug was subjected to night after night of verbal abuse and threats. Working in shifts, the prisoners would shout across the courtyard dividing their part of the prison from Doug's. Insults included threats against his family, accompanied by strings of expletives.

Dave was Doug's cell mate. His sleep was of course non-existent during this period, although he was not the actual target of the victimization. Dave had become a Christian a few weeks before, and he suggested to Doug that he ask David for some advice. Doug duly sent in a wing application, and David went down to see him late one afternoon.

As David entered the room he realized he was dealing with a very troubled man. Doug's torment was proving unbearable. Sitting up, he brushed back his silver-grey hair. Although short in stature he didn't have the appearance of one easily intimidated, but David could see that he looked a lot older than his 50 years, probably the effect of the continual abuse he was now suffering.

'Can you help me?' asked Doug in a desperate tone. 'I don't think I can take this much more.'

David listened carefully as sorrow and fear poured out of this terrified man's lips. Doug declared himself innocent of his alleged crimes and David did not argue. Many of the men protested against their imprisonment or their sentence.

Pleading innocent was the norm. David often half-joked that he had 350 innocent men under his care! Nevertheless we knew that some of the men were indeed innocent of all or part of their indictments, and that stitch-ups were a reality of life for part of the criminal world. For this reason David left the judgements to God, supported by what he felt was sound biblical backing, and dealt with the more immediate needs of each individual he met. After he had prayed with David it was obvious there was a sense of relief in Doug's voice and a glimmer of brightness in his eyes.

'So this is what Dave, my cell mate, was talking about,' said Doug. 'I sure feel different but I don't know why.'

Douglas certainly looked calmer, but David realized that his present anguish would continue unless something could be done about the aggression from 'F' wing.

David had two options. Firstly, he could request that this man be moved to another establishment on compassionate grounds, although of course the grapevine would inevitably catch up with him, and his flight prove pointless – furthermore, the man would then be beyond David's further assistance. Secondly, he could report the incident and attempt to pin down the perpetrators. This option was fraught with problems, not least of which was the possibility of an intensification of hostilities.

David thought for a moment, when into his mind slipped an amazing third suggestion. Praying silently for courage, he faced Doug and said confidently, 'We're going to ask God to help you, Doug.

I'm going to pray that angels will watch over you. We need a real miracle here.'

The bewildered inmate looked hopefully towards the chaplain.

'Is this possible?' Doug whispered. He had certainly never heard of any such thing before, but then he had never heard of praying to God and feeling a real buzz from it before either. He decided to go with it.

'Can you do that?' David's faith that he should act on this idea did not waver, but he later admitted he would have appreciated a change of orders at that particular moment if it had been possible ...

David stood up to pray and asked God to post two of his largest angels in that cell – one at the door and one at the window. His prayer grew with confidence as he spoke, and by the time he said Amen his conviction was solid.

The next morning David visited Doug in his cell.

'You'll never believe what happened,' enthused the excited inmate as David entered the room. 'There wasn't a sound last night. No sound at all. I slept right through for the first time in weeks.'

David gave a broad cheerful smile and sat down on the hard bed.

'That's just great, Doug,' he said. 'I think we had better say a prayer of thanks, don't you?'

'Oh yes,' replied a very grateful Doug. 'I really do, it's truly amazing.'

'I had an angel in my Peter, a real angel,' said Doug ['Peter' is prison slang for a cell, after Peter's enforced stay in prison]. From that moment on there were no more threats or abuse hurled towards Doug's cell, and he and his cell mate had much to talk about. Doug was greatly affected by this event and brought inmate after inmate to David's attention in the following weeks.

There were many other such amazing incidents of a seemingly coincidental nature. But, as they say, although answers to prayer may seem coincidental, strange occurrences stop when the prayer does. Here we were covered by prayer and involved in a very real front-line ministry, and God's help was just flowing on and on.

Pete, for instance, was adamant that he didn't want God as he had no evidence that God existed. He decided to throw down the gauntlet, which in our dealings with God, is often a very rash thing to do.

'I'll believe if my sister chooses to visit me,' he said firmly.

Pete and his sister June had fallen out many years before. June lived in a sleepy Devon village many miles and thoughts away from East Sussex. Now that Peter was inside he had time to reflect on his lost years of sibling contact, and regretted the fact they didn't talk. Real people are unable to resolve their differences as easily as characters in soap operas do week by week. Perhaps that's why we all like to watch the neighbours in Ramsay Street apologizing to each other regularly and sincerely, because we know in reality that people will hold on to resentments, jealousies and slights for many a decade, and even die without resolving the festering wounds, usually caused by the tiniest of incidents. Indeed, soap-watching could be perceived as a national exercise in wishful thinking!

Pete obviously wished this awkward silence with his sister could be broken, and he was adamant nothing could be changed and that he'd only consider God if it did. Three weeks later his bluff was called – June turned up to visit him.

David met up with Pete the next day, and he was so overwhelmed and overjoyed that he responded instantly to the offer of a new start with God. Days later he was still seen shaking his head with disbelief, but with a tiny smile on the edge of his lips that would burst into a full toothy grin whenever David walked down the wing.

'It's amazing,' said Pete to anyone who would listen, 'just amazing.'

Roy met a relative of a prisoner one day outside the prison walls. He had gone out to his van to pick up a book he'd promised to show an inmate, when he looked past the rows of cars neatly parked in the drive and saw a woman sitting under a large tree, which stood on a slope leading down to the main road.

Roy was concerned, because the woman was curled up with her head between her knees, and appeared to be crying. As he approached her, however, he realized there were no sobs or indications that the woman was in distress, but he felt he should speak to her anyway, and ventured, 'Hello, can I help you?'

The woman started and glanced up at Roy. He sensed she was a little alarmed at this disturbance, and aware that his muscular appearance might well have given her extra cause for concern, he added quickly, 'I'm a member of the chaplaincy department in the prison. We are available to help people. Are you all right?'

The woman pushed her long hair back from her face and explained, 'I'm praying. My brother is inside the prison and I don't know what else to do. I came here to visit him but when I arrived I just felt I should sit under this tree first and pray for him.'

Roy spoke to the woman for a while, and promised that the team would look out for her relative. Then the woman stood up and went into the prison to visit her wayward brother.

The next morning Craig became a Christian, and was able to ring his sister to tell her the good news.

'And all because a woman sat beneath a tree to pray,' reported Roy that afternoon. 'It really was quite a coincidence, wasn't it?' said Roy, winking, knowing full well it was more than that.

'A real coincidence indeed!' David answered.

One Sunday after the morning service, David was walking through the wings with a message for an inmate. Suddenly a man called out to him across the landing. David saw a thin, dishevelled inmate leaning against his cell entrance and motioning him to come across. David duly approached the man, whose name was Jordan, and asked, 'How can I help you?'

Jordan eyed the chaplain up and down, and David was not quite sure whether he was approving or not of this man he had summoned to his assistance.

'I'm not a religious man,' Jordan began. David took little notice of this opener because inmates and officers used it so often that its impact was negligible. This morning he didn't even respond with his usual, 'God is aware of that.' The comment was usually followed by an excuse as to why its user had not been in the habit of attending church, though seldom, in David's experience, did it mean 'I don't believe in God'.

Jordan went on, 'Well, as I said, I'm not religious at all, but since I've been in here I've been thinking. I'd like to get to know God. I've tried to get to chapel but I've never made it somehow.'

David knew that some of the inmates found getting to chapel a problem. It always meant putting your name down the day before, and often missing other tempting activities. Sometimes there were limits to numbers too.

'Anyway,' continued Jordan, 'I've been praying in here,' indicating his cell, 'and I felt I was meant to stand outside here and ask the next bloke who came along.' He gazed up at David as if looking for a reaction, but waited only a second before adding, 'and it was you! So could you help me find God ... at all?' he finished, almost lamely.

So David prayed with Jordan, and a volunteer later read the Bible with him and taught him to pray. He grew as a Christian quite swiftly, and displayed a real drive to find a new purpose for his life. His faith had obviously been kickstarted that Sunday morning on the wing.

We were surrounded by remarkable things happening to the men, and often amazed how God used events to spur us on in our own faith. A day late last year was one of these rather special events. David and I were in a train returning from London, and it was about midnight. We were chatting about the evening we'd just experienced. David had been invited to speak to the Christian fellowship at the Houses of Parliament. As well as committed Christians there had been many interested guests – to say it was an honour and a thrill to have been there is a gross understatement. We were really on a high. In spite of obvious nerves we had felt so up-lifted by prayer that the whole event had gone like a dream. We had met Douglas Hurd, Lord Longford, Emma Nicholson and numerous other household names at the buffet held in the Speaker's apartments. David had spoken well and clearly, and had pulled no punches about the need to change men's hearts if we really wanted a drop in the crime rate, stating that no amount of tinkering with sentencing policy would make the slightest difference to men who felt that a request 'not to do it again because we, the middle class, don't like it' was an insufficient reason to start going straight.

It was a bold speech, and we had felt we must be true to what we really believed. I had drafted the speech with great care after we had talked at length together about this opportunity, and David had put across the message in his usual witty and anecdotal style.

I had watched him delivering his speech, standing in front of a vast and impressive fireplace, with the rows of chairs facing him, each with an elegant and important person seated upon it. The lifesize portraits of former Speakers looked down from high on the walls, and the rich red and gold décor formed a stylish setting for this impressive scene.

The huge banqueting table was covered with plates from the preceding meal, and everyone there was remarkably attentive, listening to this ordinary chaplain who was used to addressing a very different audience.

David relaxed into the talk, and as usual took questions from the floor with both ease and humour. Asked about officers he responded with a story about one who had recently approached him about his fear of dying. David told how he had taken the man's fear seriously, and reminded him that it was well founded, as statistically one out of one people die ... David went on to explain that he had firmly, but kindly, confronted the officer with the Gospel's message – 'Those who believe go to Heaven. Those who don't have chosen Hell.' The listeners, almost hanging on every word by now, were relieved by David's revelation that the officer chose at this point to become a Christian.

In the vote of thanks an elderly and obviously experienced member thanked David heartily for his forthright yet humorous approach, and expressed a wish that more clerics would be as clear and direct in their message.

We were greatly relieved. The straight approach could have backfired but it didn't. Each guest had heard the Gospel clearly that night, as well as learning what was happening to the inmates and staff of Lewes Prison. The opportunity was one given to very few, and we could only pray it would have lasting and meaningful effects. Sufficient to say that Viscount Brentford, who as Chairman of the organization had sent us the invitation, was thrilled with the occasion and reported that many had felt they had had a thoroughly good and stimulating evening. We thanked our prayer partners in our hearts as we left that building, and could hardly believe where this work had led us.

So obviously on the train that night our conversation was centring round the events and conversations of the evening, when we were suddenly interrupted. We were in a carriage with a corridor running beside it, and suddenly there was a sharp tapping on the window. We looked up, breaking off in mid-sentence, and sat upright as we rather nervously found ourselves staring at a young, dirty face looking at us through the glass. Behind that face stood the taller, heftier frame of a second young man, also peering in at us too. The first man placed his hand on the door handle and began to open it. By now we could see his rather untidy style of dress and the tattoo just below his right eye.

He stared at us and fixed his gaze on David 'Where do I know you from?' he asked. Though our hearts were thumping, there was a tone in his voice that indicated he was not really threatening us.

David thought quickly. He knew he must respond with care. 'Lewes?' he replied. 'Do I know you from Lewes?'

He deliberately only referred to the town in case his first feelings were wrong, but he need not have worried.

'Lewes Prison,' responded the young man. '*That's* where I know you from. You're the Father, ain't you? The Father in the prison. Here, Mick.' With this, he stuck his head back into the corridor and addressed his friend. 'It's the Father. You know, from the prison.'

The second man ventured the tiniest of smiles before retreating down the corridor. The first man opened the door of the carriage fully and stepped in. He sat down opposite David and pronounced, 'I'll have a word with you. I'll sit here.'

We had mixed feelings. At least we knew where he was from, but we still had no idea about his intentions or what he wanted to have a word with us about!

'I remember you,' he started. 'You gave me a radio. I was desperate. All alone. You gave me a radio.' He grinned from ear to ear obviously recalling the situation.

'You gave me a radio ... and I've still got it.' He triumphed almost as if it were the only item he'd managed to take care of in his short but obviously eventful life. 'They sent me to Wandsworth,' he went on. 'I was banged up 23 hours out of 24. It was hell. But I had that radio. I'll never forget that, or you,' he said looking straight at David.

'So you're out now?' said David, stating the obvious. 'What are you doing?'

'I'm out with my mate seeing a friend at Gatwick,' replied the man. 'Paul's the name. Paul. Do you remember me?'

'Well yes,' said David, 'but I had forgotten your name. Glad to be out?'

'You bet,' he responded, 'I can't get over this, you know. I haven't got a job yet but I've still got that radio. I'm off now,' he declared as swiftly as he had announced his intention to stay.

'I hope you get a job soon,' I said, as he turned and reached for the door handle. 'Good luck,' I added.

'Yeah thanks,' said Paul and slipped out to join his mate again, still muttering about the radio.

'I've never been so glad that I gave a man a radio,' said David after Paul had gone. 'It obviously meant so much to him.' He hadn't responded to the Gospel as far as we knew, but he had to a simple act of kindness.

'Someone gave us the money for that radio,' mused David. 'They'll never know what they did.'

Then we started talking about the irony of this event: the Houses of Parliament one moment, an ex-inmate on the train the next. Kipling's poem, 'If', about being able to talk both to princes and the common man, sprang to mind.

We knew that here was our real calling – of course, we had thoroughly enjoyed the glamour and excitement of the evening, but nothing could beat the thrill of offering the Good News of Jesus to men like Paul, or the joy of knowing that the simple gift of a cheap little radio in the name of Jesus could have such a profound and lasting effect. We knew too that when we all face God we will be answerable as much for those tiny things we do as we will be for the greater events of our lives. It is in the giving of a cup of water to a stranger that our real faith is revealed.

CHAPTER 5

✳

The Defence Team

Working with prisoners is exciting and satisfying. It can also be tough and frustrating. There have been times when the frustration of being unable to meet both the demands and the opportunities of the ministry has been almost demoralizing. A never-ending stream of new inmates coming into the prison and responding to the Gospel sometimes meant we didn't have proper time to cover their needs. Criticisms that there was no point in offering people a change if we couldn't follow it up, so that they became lasting disciples, were often expressed by those we believed should have been more open to a move of God, and who would have done better by offering a hand of help rather than an unconstructive put-down.

But those who chose to get to know these prisoners found that in spite of the difficulties of bringing men into a growing faith, the rewards of the activity were huge. As in any Christian work people have fallen by the wayside, and many have stagnated in their faith. After all, outside we often meet Christians we have known for years who appear to have gone no further down the road to commitment than when they first believed. So it is for some of the Christian inmates, and we believe the principles of the parable of the sower apply equally to a prison ministry as they do to any outside church.

> While a large crowd was gathering and people were coming to Jesus from town after town, he told this parable: 'A farmer went out to sow his seed. As he was scattering the seed, some fell along the path; it was trampled on, and the birds of the air ate it up. Some fell on rock, and when it came up, the plants withered because they had no moisture. Other seed fell among thorns, which grew up with it and choked the plants. Still other seed fell on good soil. It came up and yielded a crop, a hundred times more than was sown.'
>
> When he said this he called out, 'He who has ears to hear, let him hear.'   (Luke 8:4–8)

If the seed represents the Word of God in the form of the Good News of Jesus, just how often and how intensively have we taken part in the spreading of it? We yearn to bring people to Jesus Christ, but if we're honest, we often work to help those we love the most and those to whom we are more readily drawn, with little real desire to help those less attractive. In our work we often meet those who pay lip service to the need to evangelize widely, but who feel it is not their own calling, and who are not prepared to enter into any commitment to it, be that in a prison, a housing estate or overseas.

The seed that fell on the path came to nothing, and all those who have decided to respond to the call to evangelize will know that a proportion of seed will fall into the lives of those who show no interest at all in the things of God. In the prison this is a reality too.

'No thanks mate,' said Bill, who had sat through a clear and concise presentation of the Gospel in chapel one morning. 'I don't want to offend you,' he said to David, who had just asked him if he wanted God to help him in his life.

'You haven't offended me,' replied David, 'you have offended God, but then you will answer to him one day and not to me.'

Bill was taken aback but still resolved that the cost of discipleship was too high for him.

Steve was another case in point.

'I believe all roads lead to God,' he stated when asked a similar question. 'I believe in a life force, an energy – I'll plug into that.' For him the Gospel had fallen on a barren path and the uniqueness of Christ passed him by.

Some of the seed in the story fell on rock and began to grow, but withered because there was no moisture to keep it going. Every work of evangelism will meet the people represented by this type of ground. When I was younger I was part of a flourishing Bible-based youth group that met the needs of hundreds of teenagers, and urged them to submit their lives to God's service. Over 20 years later it is obvious that a fair number of those teenagers never went on to maturity of faith. No leader to whom I have spoken will dare to hazard a guess as to which characters in their present groups will come into this category, but they are sadly forced to admit that there will be some. Only God knows people's hearts, and we cannot presume to say this one will stay the course rather than that one. It is not for us to know, and we prejudge at our own peril because we are clearly warned in Scripture not to do so.

Jim responded to the Gospel one Sunday in the service because he felt he needed help in his life. He prayed as all the others had done, and said that he felt the power of God inside as David ministered to him. Nevertheless he was already wavering by the next week, and by the following Sunday he was not only missing from chapel but said he no longer wished to have chaplaincy visits.

Why did this happen? It is rare for someone to slip away so swiftly, but it does occur, although we could see no reason why Jim's heart was such stony ground. There was no difference in his approach that could be discerned, and we were left with no satisfactory explanation.

Of course we were disappointed, but what should we say at this point – 'Let's give up? People like this don't understand enough. Stop the ministry. Don't preach the Good News'? No, because this parable prepares us for the possibility of it happening. Inevitably, some will respond with what seems a very real initial commitment, but they will still fall away.

Other seed fell among the thorns, which grew up with it and choked it. Mark's gospel adds that because of these weeds the seed could not bear fruit. This ground represents the ineffectual Christian who has experienced the things of God and enjoys the benefits of a clear conscience and the hope of heaven, but whose life is filled with other activities which allow no room for maturity of faith or service of others.

Toby became a Christian, and he appeared regularly in chapel on a Sunday, where he sang lustily, prayed unselfconsciously, and chatted to visitors gladly. Nevertheless, he showed little interest in prayer and Bible study on the wing, and his peer group appeared to dominate his activity. None of his friends turned up in chapel with him. They thought Toby just needed a Sunday fix of religion, and knew it had little effect on his everyday existence. Now of course we hope that the spark in Toby will grow to a flame, but we are concerned for him on his release, because only a deep and conscious commitment will keep him on track on 'the out'.

Nevertheless, the seed that fell on good ground yielded a good crop – a hundred times larger than the original. Here is the crux of this parable. We tend to focus on the first three types of ground and major on the negative aspects, but the truth is that we are meant to recognize the joy of the fruitfulness of the seed on the good ground.

The true Christian not only finds God and his peace, but goes on to give service by bringing others to a similar experience. Fruitfulness is the key to reality. If there is no fruit there is no real life in one's faith. This message is a two-edged sword, of course, being both a huge encouragement and an immense challenge.

At this point the strong converts among the inmates come into their own. Yes, we meet those who falter along the way or even fall at the first hurdle, but we are also privileged to meet those who are 'the good ground'. Some of our men cause us to cringe in embarrassment when we compare our faith and willingness to declare the Gospel with theirs.

Mark brought eight or more of his fellow prisoners to the chapel. He was a young man who found faith when he was weighed down by his own failure and lifestyle. I'd met him in the chapel, and he had told me that his Mum always went to church. He committed his life that morning and rang to tell her the good news. Her prayers and thanks must have been very profound, because her 'lost' son came home at last.

Similarly Graham found faith and wasn't afraid to share it. He told many on the wings of his new love for God, and began to express himself and his new faith in writing. One Sunday he burst into chapel and approached David with a piece of paper. 'Can I read it?' he asked, waving the piece of paper in front of his nose.

David looked at the keen, dark-haired young man before him, and saw his enthusiasm. 'What is it?' he asked, gently taking the writing from Graham's hands.

'My poem,' declared Graham. 'It tells what God means to me now. I wrote it myself. I can't stop writing now.' Then he added confidently, 'I know it by heart, you know. I don't need the paper.'

David was sorry to disappoint such keenness, but there was a band in that morning and the schedule was really tight. 'Look, Graham. It will have to be next week. You can read it next week, I promise.'

The look of disappointment on Graham's face was touching. He was a good-looking fellow, and made the best of himself even in prison. He would not have been out of place in any church setting that morning, and he displayed a surprising maturity. Normally inmates want everything 'now', and they are unable to be patient about anything. If one has promised to do something or bring something, they will badger almost hourly until the promise has been fulfilled. Maybe having nothing and being out of control of one's own actions almost wrings this attitude out of them. Suffice it to say it is almost universally the case.

Graham somehow mustered up the willpower to be patient that Sunday and said, 'OK. OK, I'll wait. I wanted to do it. I really did. I'll practise. I'll be good. I'll do it next week.'

All week Graham practised in his cell. He read it so many times to his peers that he really did commit it fully to memory. The next Sunday he was up as early as he was able, reminding us that his turn had come.

'Where's the paper, then, Graham?' asked David.

'Oh, I don't need that,' replied the now impatient inmate, 'I know it by heart.'

'I think you'll need it when you get up there,' said David confidently. 'It's different at the front.'

Graham hesitated. He hadn't thought of that.

'You'll have to wait another week,' said David, frightened that the prisoner would stumble and be demoralized by his performance. A look of utter dejection crossed Graham's face and once again he took his place amongst the empty chairs. But, not wanting to see the lad disappointed any further, David sent a volunteer to his office, where he thought there might still be a copy of the poem on his table. He didn't want to raise Graham's hopes unduly, but hoped he could resolve the problem.

Halfway through the first hymn a breathless volunteer thrust the copy of the poem into the chaplain's hands. 'Great,' whispered David, and crept up to Graham, who was hiding his disappointment well as he sang heartily.

'Here we are, Graham,' said David pushing the paper into Graham's hands. 'You're on!'

Graham looked intensely at David, expressing his thanks with his eyes. His moment had come and he could hardly believe it.

As it happened, he really did need that copy of his poem because in spite of his enthusiasm and confidence, it was scary up there in front of everyone! He read the poem clearly and well, and grinned from ear to ear when he had finished. There was a huge round of applause and a very cheerful inmate returned to his seat.

Some weeks later, just as Kenny, an earlier inmate, had done the year before, Graham was chosen to read his poem at the prison carol service. If reading in chapel is a challenge, then doing so at this major event of the year is awesome. Lots of outside visitors come, and together with governors, officers and inmates, the congregation approaches two hundred.

David at least was prepared. In spite of his earlier experience, Graham still believed in his own ability to remember his own writing. Had he not pronounced it a hundred times since that Sunday in chapel, and without mistakes? Surely he could do it now?

David had placed a copy of the poem on the lectern 'just for appearances', he had told Graham, but when the moment came Graham froze, and was intensely grateful to see that typed sheet in front of him.

When he closed, he raised his palm in acknowledgement of the applause and the cries of 'Go for it, Graham' and 'Well done, mate' which accompanied it.

Here is Graham's poem, which he is pleased to share with everyone who will listen. I am sure you will agree with all who have heard it before that it is a real and moving expression of one man's faith.

ALL THIS FOR ME

I once lay in a tomb of life, dead to rhyme and
    reason,
All purpose gone, no hope of goal, blind
    without a vision.
The walls were made to keep you out, instead
    they kept me in.
The stone was there to keep me safe, to hide
    away my sin.

A small still voice kept telling me, 'I have life for
    you,
I really want to set you free, to let you start
    anew,'
But I felt safe within the dark, the light I could
    not bear.
The fact that Jesus died for me was neither here
    nor there.

The mask I wore was made of pride, to hide my
    haunts and fears
I wore an air of confidence, water-logged in
    tears,
With mouth and eyes in conflict, I tried to play
    the part.
I didn't want the world to know I had a broken
    heart.

One day a man from Nazareth came knocking
    at my door.
'I've come to set you free, my son, and give you
    so much more.'
'But Lord!' I cried, 'can this be true? my chains
    are very tight.'
'Peace, be still, come, follow me, you'll find my
    yoke is light.'

I left my tomb and followed him, and very soon
    I found
That all my sins and hurts and fears, no longer
    had me bound.
My blinded eyes were opened, my shackled
    heart was free,
The liberator, Jesus, has done all this for me!
               'Greatest Love'

                Graham Pinsent
                October 1996

David read a book by Romanian pastor Richard Wurmbrand, and was struck by the point that 'there is no "I" in the Our Father' – he and I know that without others we can neither sustain nor expand the ministry. Of course we are not a church and have no paid personnel, but we know each person can bring a distinct contribution to what is taking place, and that we are totally dependent on volunteers to disciple the new converts.

In *The Cross Between Thieves*, our first team members are recalled and many, though not all, are still with us at this time. However, new people spring up too, and help to expand and enhance the work. Andy, from YWAM, was one of these, and he began to come in on Sundays and to work once a week with inmates. He found he needed to reassess his approach to pastoring situations, as the men were often lacking in literacy skills and unused to reasoned argument, but he enjoyed his ministry and was a fruitful contact for many prisoners.

Jim Greenwood, a real friend from earlier days, began to come in to chapel once a fortnight, and to offer his skills and his faith to pray with inmates moments after their prayers of commitment. Travelling some 50 miles did little to daunt his valuable enthusiasm and, always a man of great prayer, he contributed greatly to the services. For his part, the work ministered to his spirit in a real way, as he had often toiled in the Lord's service in difficult home and church situations and had shown steadfastness well beyond most others. The excitement of seeing the men's response he viewed as God's reward to him, and felt privileged to be part of it all. Furthermore, his infectious laugh and sense of perspective were a huge asset to the group, and we were delighted to have him aboard.

David definitely had great faith in Jim's abilities, and soon grew to pass new converts on to him for prayer. One morning Robert came to faith, and told David he had been playing with the occult on a small-time basis. David summoned Jim and a volunteer to pray with the man. 'He needs to have prayer for release,' he told the solemn Jim.

'Right,' was the answer, and a faithful Jim said prayers with the volunteer over the man, to cast out any evil influence that might have entered him.

'He was so authoritive in prayer,' said the volunteer later, when we were all settled in the chapel with a mug of tea after the inmates had returned to their wings.

'That's good,' said David. 'So you have had lots of experience of this type of thing, Jim?'

A huge smile spread across Jim's face, and his shoulders began to shake as he explained, 'Oh no, I've never done anything like it before. I've never made it to the right team or been sent on a relevant course, but I knew I had to do it. I couldn't let you down... It all seems so right, so obvious and almost, well ordinary,' he continued. 'I guess I really am just learning on the job and where better would I do that?'

We had also developed links with local bands and groups who would attend a service and brighten it up considerably. Because the inmates moved so often, there was no stable community, and each service on a Sunday (or indeed each week on the wings) was unique. Consequently, as long as we knew in advance and there was an element of real commitment by the Christians, we could live comfortably with many short-term visitors.

For example, Terry Tully, a local man who used a sketch board to preach, could establish a meaningful ministry with just one visit every two months – each occasion he visited was equally as valid and valuable.

However, although Sundays were normally well catered for, we had times when only four of us were there and when we were really stretched to meet the needs of the inmates. Still, we had to trust that we had the right people, and leave our concerns in the hands of God.

At Icthus Church in London we met Graham Kendrick, who expressed a real interest in our work. When he began his ministry he sang in pubs and clubs in order to evangelize. As a student in the seventies, I had enjoyed his early tapes, and greatly appreciated songs such as 'Paid on the Nail' and 'No room at the world'.

I chatted to Graham about these songs, and he seemed amused I could remember these very 'ancient writings'. He obviously had a heart for evangelism with the unchurched, and agreed to visit the prison in the next few months.

The week before Graham's visit, David told the men that he was coming.

'Who's he?' asked an inquisitive inmate.

'Well, he's really famous,' replied David, realizing instantly that this was a hopeless task.

'Is he that bloke who plays the guitar on 'A' wing?' asked another.

'No,' responded David, 'he's coming down from London to play for you.'

'Well, that's good of 'im,' interjected a third, leaning back in his chair and placing his hands behind his head. 'I like music and guitars.'

Graham arrived at the prison by 7.45 a.m., and I met him and his companion outside. I thanked them for coming, and knocked on the huge gate to gain entrance. The officer on duty let us in, and began to look with suspicion at Graham's equipment.

Slightly flustered, Graham handed his mobile phone co-operatively to the officer behind the screen.

'Oh good,' teased the officer. 'I need to make a few calls to Australia this morning.'

Graham smiled, realizing this was unlike the usual welcome he received in churches across the country!

The second officer was searching his guitar case. 'These yours?' he questioned, picking out a set of spare guitar strings from beneath the splendid instrument.

'Yes,' replied Graham, 'they're spare guitar strings.'

'Great for this,' declared the officer, drawing his finger across his throat in a mock attempt at suicide. 'I don't think we'll have those in, do you?'

Graham looked aghast at the suggestion, and asked, 'What do I do if I break a string?'

'Come back and see me,' responded the officer, who was warming to the task.

We had all learned a long time before to go with the general banter and teasing of the officers. They had a huge responsibility to handle, and often carried the can for being either too lax or too strict with the interpretation of the rules.

Humour is a huge reliever of tension, and it is certainly rife in Lewes. David always thoroughly enjoys it all, and certainly gives as good as he gets whenever he can. Graham Kendrick was obviously also learning fast, and a glimmer of a smile spread across his features as, horror of horrors, the officer found a 'secret' compartment in the guitar case that lifted up to reveal his screw driver, kept on hand to alter his strings whenever necessary.

Without a word the officer held up the offending item, raised his eyebrows and slowly handed it over at the desk. 'Have a good morning,' he said as he passed the guitar back to its owner.

Graham came up to the chapel and soon felt at home, in spite of the missing typed order of service which apparently other organizers always gave him.

David joked, 'OK, Graham, how's your playing on "Majesty"?'

Graham looked surprised. 'Majesty?' he asked, 'why Majesty?'

'Well, because we always play Majesty, and anyway it's the only one in our book that you haven't written, so you need the practice.'

Graham grinned, and realized that this environment was rather more easy going than usual, and definitely different from the norm!

We did always play Majesty – everyone could sing it, and everyone did sing it, both in chapel and out. It is a deep song easily sung by men, and not very musical men at that.

One day David was stopped outside the prison by a man he failed to recognize.

'Do you remember me?' a voice asked.

David looked back and saw a man sitting on a bench, either having visited or about to visit an inmate inside the prison. Unfortunately David could not recall the man's name.

'Will this help?' asked the man, and with that he began to sing the words of Majesty. The scales fell from David's eyes and with a grin he declared, 'John, John Drake, I remember you.'

David shook his hand, and John went on to tell David how he was now out and living nearby.

'I still can't read very well,' he confided, 'but I can still sing Majesty. When we went to the other prison all of us Lewes men used to sing Majesty. I even asked for it in chapel once, but no one else let us sing it there. I'll never forget that song. I sing it when I want to go back to my old ways.'

So Graham was required to play Majesty that morning he visited the chapel, but he did have to check the chords first! He was brilliant when his turn came to play and sing, and the men were really moved.

Afterwards a man came forward in order to respond to God, and Graham was thrilled to talk to him and show him a new Bible.

After that Graham popped down several times over the months, and each time he saw men become Christians. It was obviously a pleasure to be unknown, to be there on the cutting edge of evangelism, and to see his own songs inspire faith there and then in individual prisoners.

How about us? Well, we were honoured to have him, and so pleased that the men were having this opportunity to hear a man of such talent singing the Gospel to them.

Similarly we are thrilled to have visitors from many churches, who back us in prayer and support so fruitfully. Sending visitors is of course a great help to us, but of even more meaningful assistance is their level of enthusiasm and encouragement. Several individuals are a positive and sustaining influence on us, and we realize how much benefit we derive from the simplest call, letter or visit if it emanates from genuine concern to support and motivate.

We believe this area of forging supporting links will be one of growth for us, and we pray that people will be drawn not only into our own work, but into work with prisoners in general.

The need is great and the workers so few, but those who are involved have gained great benefit from it. I picture all the people who help us as if they were a defence team in a court of law, fighting to give the prisoners a chance, not to escape responsibility but to have a new start. Our plea is that it is not a hopeless cause in which we are engaged, but rather that it is possible for prisoners to find God and make a real contribution, both to the Church and to society as a whole. I believe this to be a fully achievable goal, as long as we all work together to help them to do so.

CHAPTER 6

✳

Advocating Simplicity and Perseverance

'But it's just a Sunday School story,' blurted out a flustered and rather cross Martin.

'I don't wish to offend you or be critical,' he continued, rising to his task and certainly intending to be critical if not offensive.

'They all listen attentively but all you're doing is telling Bible stories – and that's all!'

The critic looked at the chaplain for a response to his comments, but for once found David rather reticent. He stood leaning against the hall listening to this rather intense inmate, wondering at his dismissive tone. Surely this man should have had more wisdom? – after all, he was a long-term Christian himself who, prior to his arrest for a serious offence, had been involved in committed Christian work.

Martin grew tired of waiting for a response, and chose instead to elaborate his opinions. 'I'm also most concerned about your follow-up methods,' he continued, obviously enjoying this expression of his previously pent up views.

David listened as Martin brought up one by one those issues which to us were the old chestnuts. It

was unusual, but by no means unique, to have
an established Christian on the wings, and David
knew that if he could be involved in the work Martin
would be of great service to the other inmates.
Focusing on the shortcomings of the system was
certainly not a productive activity for his gifts. David
spent some time with Martin trying to answer his
questions reasonably. Later he came home and
attempted to work over the conversation as cons-
tructively as possible. Our attention was soon
centred on the phrase 'it's just Sunday School', and
after due consideration we decided to take it as a
compliment.

All the talks in the chapel week by week feature
a simple Bible story, and attempt to explain it in
contemporary terms. Simply expressed messages
they certainly are, but simultaneously profound
none the less. Martin seemed to have missed the
point, because casting light on Jesus' life and
ministry must be the most beneficial thing we can
do for another person during any exposition of the
Bible. However, the notion that spiritual matters
must be complex or technical is not one unique to
Martin. Whether inadvertently or not, large parts of
the Church have rendered themselves incompre-
hensible to the man of average or below average
intelligence. By this I certainly do not mean that
traditional, more formal services are more culpable
in this matter; quite the contrary. Many regularized
services have huge benefits for the less literate
amongst the population – after all, if something is
the same each week you can at least learn it by
heart, and there is great reassurance in familiarity,

as we all know. Furthermore, an emphasis on the visual provided by the use of religious pictures, symbols and celebrations involves the use of the whole of a person's understanding, not just the mind. Even if repetitive liturgy were the problem, there is no solace to be found in those of a much freer habit condemning traditional worship out of hand, because they too fiercely maintain their own ritual, albeit a more expressive and less predictable one. No, I believe we are all equal in this area, since any church, whatever its persuasion, is capable of exclusivity and a non-welcoming culture.

Rick came back inside after maintaining nearly a year outside trouble free. 'I'm so sorry to be back,' he gasped, grabbing hold of David's arm, 'but it's good to see you. Will you help me again? I'll be up in chapel. I do enjoy the services.'

David welcomed Rick back, although obviously sad to see him return, but realizing what an uphill struggle he had faced.

'Did you go to church, Rick?' he asked quietly. 'How did it go?'

'Oh yes,' said the dark-haired and very untidy inmate, 'I did. I used to go to this church in Sussex and I wanted to talk to him [here he motioned upwards] but I weren't allowed.'

'What do you mean?' questioned David in a rather concerned voice.

'Well,' continued Rick, chattering on, blissfully unaware of the effect this was having, 'I was asked to leave. "Here you, get out of here," one bloke said, and even when I kept trying I was always asked to go. I don't know why,' he finished lamely.

'Oh dear,' replied David, 'I am so sorry.'

He knew that Rick looked particularly dishevelled, but he was also sure that he wanted a new future for himself. What a shame he had felt so rejected.

Rick began to continue his news, 'I didn't have anywhere to go on the out. I can't read much and I needed help. They gave me a room, but I didn't have anywhere to sit. I know I shouldn't have done it, but I stole to get a chair. Can anyone help me next time?' he asked innocently.

David certainly prayed that someone would help him next time, and we resolved to link him up properly on his release and point him in the way of Howard, who used to look after him during his previous spell inside. Hopefully, Howard would help him on the outside as well.

We knew that educating the outside churches was growing into a priority area. Christians are obviously scared of ex-inmates, and find their lifestyles and habits unsuitable bed-fellows for their own preferences. Nevertheless, unless we can persuade churches to 'adopt' our men then many will fall by the wayside, and that would be a tragedy.

One day I was incensed by a Christian's suggestion that we couldn't expect churches to pick up these people without training. Although this person was a lecturer in a theological college, the idea that we can only minister if we have undergone a course on a specific area is a fallacy. Which Bible do people read, I wondered? The disciples, who were aware of being uneducated men, went about ministering to vast numbers of people, most of whom were from the lower layers of society. What training did they receive, apart from being with Jesus? It seems that training, although a helpful and valid activity, can sometimes be thought to replace simple discipleship and obedience to God's commands to help people. Of course we need schooling and advice, but there is nothing like learning on the job, and if an absence of specific training means the neglect of whole groups of society, on the grounds that we cannot relate to them, then it is an offence to the power of the Gospel. Stepping into the unknown with God is true evidence of faith, not least in the area of relationships with people to whom we are not naturally drawn.

Speaking about the work therefore has become a central part of our timetable, and we find a real response among many groups of Christians. We want to reassure people that a willingness of heart is the only criterion necessary to welcome the majority of ex-offenders who have declared an interest in the Christian faith.

As part of this aspect of ministry we began to look for Bible passages from which to start, and of course we didn't have to look very hard at all. The Bible is crammed full of references to people put into prison for every reason you can think of. Once one begins to look, the information is everywhere – Joseph falsely accused of sexual assault; Samson seized and incarcerated; John the Baptist imprisoned for speaking out; Peter and Paul caught for being Christians. These particular examples were innocent of their crimes, but there are also plenty of references to criminals who were guilty, not least of whom was Moses, who went from being a murderer to being the deliverer of God's chosen people out of Egypt.

Running alongside these stories are numerous general commands to remember, visit and help those in prison, and it would probably prove very fruitful to take note of all these references. Work with prisoners takes little time to justify from the Scriptures. The theme is starkly present.

So passages began to come to mind to use in outside talks, and a favourite was that of Jonah. He was in a prison of sorts, albeit inside a whale, and he learned to face up to God and his responsibilities whilst there. He had not wanted to spread the good news of forgiveness to the people of Nineveh, on the grounds that ... well, when we analyse the grounds they are surely staggering. It appears he did not want to tell the people of that great city to repent, on the grounds that they would respond and then God would forgive them! Here we have displayed the tragedy of the true state of many of our hearts. If we do tell 'the undesirables' about God then they might respond, be accepted and become, horror of horrors, equal to us! 'The Church isn't for people who commit crimes and go to prison, or who live on the streets, or who sell their bodies for money, is it? I don't want them in my "club". It's for people like me, after all.' Now, we may not say this openly, but there is a degree of truth in it. Perhaps we find it easy to criticize when strange or previously evil people convert, because we don't really want it to be true. Just as in the story of the prodigal son, we are the elder brother, jealous of the younger son's return to favour because we were there all the time, and can't see why his restoration now should be celebrated. Even worse maybe is that element of Pharisee about us that will always despise the tax collector, and resist his rise at any cost.

Jonah, however, came out of the whale. He repented and realized his own inadequacy, and went back to do his task. True enough the people of Nineveh repented, and, in spite of all his lessons, Jonah sulked when they did. God had, even then, to remind him that he loved every man and woman equally, and that Jonah's prejudice had no place in God's plans at all.

David tells this story to various churches, lacing it heavily with illustrations about prisoners' lives and responses to the Gospel. Always very funny, the talks draw people to listen, and the punchline or real message is very straight and simple to get across when people are so receptive.

'Are you still in the whale?' David asks, 'or are you ready to go where God sends you, whether that's abroad or to a hospital or a drug rehabilitation centre or the streets, or even to a prison?' Nearly everyone leaves with a desire not to be stuck in their own particular whale, and hopefully with a yearning to find out just where they will go next. If they come away with an interest in or a care for prison work, then that is a huge bonus, and many splendid people go on to offer practical and prayer support through such meetings. It certainly is good to open up the ministry to the outside as much as we can.

Meanwhile, back in the prison we continue picking up Bible passages that are relevant to the men, and explaining them on Sunday mornings. The two builders who chose to erect their houses on either rock or sand in Matthew 7 become two inmates called Brussel and Sprout. They are released and one can't wait to get things going the way they used to be, while the other tries to remember what he has learned about God and put it into practice. Using two chairs as 'inmates' the story is told and the point made. For weeks afterwards the men talk about Brussel and Sprout – the names proving to have been a real inspiration.

The story of Elijah and Baal is expounded, with questions as to why Elijah was not called Remand, so that the story would have been renamed as the tale of Bail and Remand! However, the serious side of choosing whom to serve is forcefully made, and several men respond in faith.

The message of Naaman is frequently chosen because it brings up the idea of doing something very ordinary to find God, namely dipping oneself in the smelly old Jordan, as that officer had to in order to cure his leprosy. Had not his own country got superior rivers after all? Have we not also got far 'superior' ways of finding meaning than just trusting God? The trouble is they all fail when the chips are down – only simple faith in God will carry you through.

So it goes on – taking these stories and showing how they all point to the one and only true helper:

Jesus. Whether they come from the Old or New Testament, the messages all point to our need of God and his ability to help us and, used as illustrations, they serve us much better than any amount of long-winded explanations would ever do.

'Are you doing the story today, David?' asked a very keen inmate one Sunday. 'I do hope so. We talk about them afterwards on the wing, you know. We tell the ones who couldn't come. They all want to hear the stories. They're really good.'

David received the praise cheerfully, because he knows we never have to make up any story or concoct a sermon for the morning, because lifting the message straight from the Bible seems to be effective every time. If people think they are 'just Bible stories' then fair enough, because that's exactly what they are, and if that medium is the best way to explain the love of God to people, then that's what we will prepare. Perhaps it would be good if in some places the practice of retelling Bible stories was restored in ordinary church life, because certainly we find a message expressed in that way is understood and retained very effectively.

Like any teaching or explaining, however, we find it necessary to cover our ground again and again. Of course we have new inmates every week, and plenty of them who have never heard the Christian message before, but even those who have responded need constant repetition of the basics. We are meeting people who have no real knowledge of Christian things at all, so it is hardly surprising really that they need a repetitious diet of knowledge and explanation. When I was at teacher training college we learned about a theorist called Bruner, who developed the concept of a spiral curriculum. This means that every time a subject is revisited one learns more about it in terms of comprehension and development. Without revisiting any area, ground is often lost and previous learning forgotten. So it is with faith. We need to revisit areas again and again, and then we slowly grow. Thus it is we celebrate Easter year by year, but no one claims to have fully grasped the meanings of its message.

The men with whom we work need considerably more 'spiral' than the average, since their starting point of understanding is often nil. Patience when dealing with offenders is paramount, and a grasp of the leaps of understanding and life changes that we require of those who come to faith is central to being able to help. Read here the story of Thomas and consider the progress he has made. Would you be willing to help a man such as this, being aware of course that he could well slip again, and need to revisit those basics many times? Whatever you feel you surely cannot help but be inspired by his obvious desire for faith and the efforts he has made to change.

I AM 37 YEARS OLD.

MY NAME IS THOMAS AND ONE DAY I WALKED INTO BRIGHTON POLICE STATION AND TOLD THEM THERE WAS A WARRENT OUT FOR MY ARREST!

NOW ILL TELL YOU THE REASON WHY I DID THAT. I WAS A RECK THROUGH

DRINK AND DRUGS, I COULD SEE NO OTHER WAY OF SAVING MY LIFE, OTHER THAN HAND MYSELF IN, I WAS A JUNKIE, WHICH I MANAGED TO GET OF AND STOP TAKING SMACK ALL TOGETHER, WITH THE HELP OF A DR FROM AN ADDICTION CENTRE, BUT I THEN STARTED TO TAKE DRINK, AND I MEAN I HIT THE DRINK LIKE NEVER BEFORE, I COULD DRINK A WHOLE CASE (24) TENNIES SUPERS 9% ALC, IN A DAY ON MY OWN, BUT NEXT DAY I WOULD NEED AND I STRESS THE WORD NEED, ONE OR TWO CANS OR SOME KIND OF DRINK JUST TO MAKE ME FEEL GOOD OR SHALL I SAY NORMAL, MOST MORNINGS I COULD NOT SHAVE BECAUSE I SHOOK THAT MUCH. THE BEST BIT, I TOLD MYSELF LIES, BY THINKING IVE GOT THIS UNDER CONTROL, BUT SOON CANS WERE NOT ENOUGH SO I STARTED DRINKING SPIRITS. DIDN'T MATTER WHAT KIND, JUST SO LONG AS I GOT DRUNK, THIS WENT ON FOR AROUND 3 MONTHS. I WAS ON THE STREETS AFTER GETTING THROWN OUT OF A NIGHT SHELTER, FOR UNKNOWINGLY TAKING AN OVERDOSE OF DRINK AND PILLS, SO ON FRIDAY THE 13.12.96 WHILE SITTING IN A DAY CENTER IN BRIGHTON, I LOOKED AROUND ME (I WAS ILL I HAD NOTHING THAT MORNING) AND THOUGHT TO MYSELF I NEED HELP

BADLY OR IM GOING TO END UP LIKE SOME OF THESE MEN, I JUST REALIZED I WAS LOSING EVERYTHING, MY RESPECT, CARE FOR MYSELF, I NEVER WASHED, I ALWAYS WORE THE SAME CLOTHES AND I STANK BADLY. WHAT MADE ME COME TO MY SENCES I WILL EXPLAIN OR AT LEAST TRY TO, OR WHAT I NOW BELIEVE TO WHAT MADE ME DO WHAT I DONE TO SAVE MYSELF, WELL I DIDNT SAVE MYSELF, I NOW BELEAVE THE LORD OUR GOD HAD A VERY BIG PART TO PLAY IN MY DOING WHAT I DID. YOU SEE AROUND 1983/84 I BECAME A BORN AGAIN CHRISTIAN, IT ONLY LASTED A FEW MONTHS BUT THAT VERY FIRST TIME I GIVE ME LIFE TO JESUS, I COULD PHISICLY FEEL THE HOLY SPIRIT SURGE THROUGH MY BODY, I WAS HIGH ON JESUS FOR A COUPLE OF WEEKS, AND I LOVED EVERY MOMENT, YOU COULDNT GET ME TO STOP TALKING ABOUT HOW REALLY GOOD I FELT, BUT SLOWLY I SLIPED BACK INTO MY OLD WAYS, AND THE THING THAT MAKES ME TRUST THE LORD HAD A HAND IN THIS CHANGE OF COARSE, WAS WAY BACK IN 83/84 WHEN I LEFT CHRIST 'HE NEVER LEFT ME' AND HE SEEN I HAD HAD ENOUGH, HE KNEW I WAS READY TO GIVE A TRUE AND (HOPEFULY) LASTING COMMITMENT TO HIM, THERE MUST BE SOME REASON FOR HIM TO DO WHAT HE DID, I DONT KNOW

WHAT AND I DONT CARE I AM JUST SO GLAD AND FILLED WITH JOY THAT HE LOOKED AFTER ME AND I NEVER KNEW UNTIL I CAME TO THIS PRISON, SO ALL YOU WHO READ THIS DONT BE LIKE ME, I NEARLY GAVE UP HOPE, AND THE SAYINGS TRUE WHERE THERE IS LIFE THERE IS HOPE THROUGH JESUS CHRIST OUR LORD.

Thomas' letter is both challenging and inspiring, isn't it? And that's exactly what he wanted it to be the day he agreed to write up his story. There are many like him who want the outside world to understand their faith, inadequate as it might sometimes be, and accept it for the reality it is for them. One thing is very clear: we may view their stumbling and struggling as a sign of weakness in faith, but they certainly don't. They pick themselves up and go on, seldom questioning whether God will take them back! Not for them the agonies and self-indulgence of wondering if they've lost their way completely – no, once they've met with God they expect him to be there for them, and are prepared to try again. This attitude is commonplace and very humbling. Similarly when things go badly they seldom seem to blame God for it – seeing even disasters as mere accidents or 'the way it is', and not stopping to question God's love because of them.

Derrick, one of our orderlies, was a lovely man who found faith in prison. He brought many to chapel, and helped numerous struggling people on the wing. However, he fell foul of a few nasty individuals who decided to 'tax' him for his own 'protection'. Derrick refused to hand over his cigarettes or phone cards, as a stand for what is right. It was a decision that cost him dear. Mixing sugar with boiling water, the men entered his cell and 'jugged' Derrick so that he was thoroughly burned, and still not content, they then set about him with two batteries in a sock until he was black and blue. Poor Derrick ended up in the hospital wing a very injured man.

The previous day David had arranged a chapel visit for Derrick and his wife, and together they had come to terms with his imprisonment and his new faith. He had been glad of the opportunity to set things straight, as he had been having some problems over a couple of his fairly large collection of children. David saw him in the hospital the day after the attack, and expected a good deal of trauma, laced with a degree of self-pity.

Derrick would have none of it. 'I am so grateful to God,' he started, looking up from his bed at the chaplain, who would hardly have been surprised to see a far more angry response. 'They missed my face,' he confirmed, pointing at his unmarked features. 'My wife would not have liked that at all. I am so glad I saw her yesterday. God is very good!'

Derrick was shipped out for his own protection, and one wonders at this man's reaction to an appalling crime. I doubt many of us would have been so ready to praise God in such a situation, but to Derrick it was just a natural response.

This simplicity of faith is not then one which succeeds due to any avoidance of trouble, but one which seems to stem from a really meaningful first encounter with God, and which remains with the new Christian through thick and thin. We Christians can certainly learn from such expressions of faith.

In terms of the courtroom theme of this book, we are indeed the briefs and advocates who must put the Christian faith in a favourable light to the world. We have to explain not only God's love, but the pathway to making a response to him. The lessons of prison ministry are clear: to be effective we must be simple in our message, being totally straightforward about the core issues, and rejecting man-made complications and barriers to faith; and we must persevere in our telling so that we do not perceive a slowly developing spiral of faith as failure but as a genuine response to God. If we can be both simple and persevering we will be encouraged by what we find, and learn to take delight in the faith of new Christians, even if their expressions of faith are far removed from our own.

Furthermore, if we feel we want to respond to these elements of Christian advocacy we must be aware that whatever we do in terms of evangelism must be given, continued and finished in an atmosphere of prayer. After all, however sound our presentation of the Gospel may be, we have to remember that we receive our remit from and must appeal ultimately to, a much higher court than any earthly one. Our guiding principle and privilege must surely be that God draws people to himself, and our role is to join him in his own work by prayer and simple obedience to the commission to spread the Good News of Jesus. When we do so the results are often amazing, and all the more so considering the inadequacy of both our prayer lives and our actions. May the stories in this book spur us on to be sound and keen advocates, because it is, after all, God's expressed work that we do.

One final story illustrates our need to reassess our attitude to explaining the Gospel. David visited a church where he was assured, 'We don't get converts here. We can't remember the last time someone came to faith.'

Although interested in the prison work and willing to support it, the members felt it had little relevance for their own ministry, which seemed to be confined to helping the faithful.

After the service one lady approached David with concern. 'I've brought a lad I know tonight. He's been before but he hasn't made a commitment.'

'Have you asked him to become a Christian?' asked David, in his usual simple style.

'Well, no,' stammered the lady, a bit taken aback, 'I haven't.'

David went over to meet the lad, who seemed very open and obviously searching. 'I found all that very interesting,' he volunteered.

David asked him directly to make a step of faith, and the young man did so at once, seemingly relieved that someone was at last going to help him through.

Later David spoke to the lady and a group of other church members. 'He's a new Christian now, look after him. You can have people find faith you know – but you do need to ask them first!'

The group, rather stunned, gathered round the boy, and seemed quite pleased, but David knew that some attitudes would have to change radically if that boy was not to remain the only person to find faith in that particular environment.

That example is rather blatant, but perhaps it points to a truth. Simple faith sharing isn't difficult, but it is costly in terms of effort and sometimes loss of face. If we want church growth perhaps many more of us must be willing to pay the price of having the courage to face possible rejection before we see the fruits of success.

CHAPTER 7

✳

Appeal to a Higher Court

Paying lip service to the power of prayer is not something in which we can afford to indulge. We know that all the response to the Gospel and the demonstration of God's power which we are privileged to witness are the result of prolonged or faith-filled prayer, and by no means only ours. Appeals to a higher court than that of an earthly authority are constantly being made by our own volunteers, friends, prayer line and the relatives of those in prison. We believe that the volume of positive answers we all receive is to demonstrate the Lordship of God over the situation, to encourage Christians and to bring ever more people to faith in Jesus.

For us the answers may seem speedy in coming, but for many, years of faith are coming to fruition as each inmate finds God for the first time. One day David received a letter from a couple who had heard about Lewes from a friend, and now wanted to find out just what was happening.

Keith had lost his way years previously, in spite of his parents' profound faith and faithfulness in commitment. Now Keith's way had resulted in his incarceration in Lewes gaol. His parents were distraught but restrained as they simply requested prayer for their beloved son. They believed he might already have been moved on, and were throwing out a life-line to David to see whether he believed there was still hope.

David looked Keith up on the inmate list, and went off to 'B' wing to find him. On his arrival, an officer told him that he thought Keith would appreciate a visit, as he was going through a hard time. David looked at the rather dishevelled and quiet inmate, and realized just what was meant by having a hard time.

'I see you've had a spot of bother,' he said to Keith, looking towards a very black and bruised eye that was obviously newly acquired.

'Yes, I have,' replied Keith, whose clear and precise speech implied that he was used to pleasanter surroundings.

'They said I'd insulted a mate ... but I don't know why ...' he finished lamely.

Keith's brush with the harsh realities of prison life had obviously shocked him, but David saw his present position as a window of opportunity in a previously solid wall of refusal.

'Your parents are very concerned about you, you know,' stated David calmly.

'You haven't told them about this eye, have you?' interjected Keith very nervously, looking anxiously up at the chaplain.

'No,' said David reassuringly. 'I didn't know you were hurt. They have been praying for you, you know.'

Keith acknowledged this first by the faintest movement of his head, and continued to listen carefully. No doubt a few days previously would have seen him hasten to show disinterest, but now he was obviously open to influence.

'It's time to let God help you, isn't it?' asked David, by now sure a positive response was possible.

'I guess so,' replied Keith, looking dazed but none the less interested.

'I believe God wants you to let him into your life, Keith. You need to become a Christian and lead a new life now,' suggested David.

'I think you're right,' conceded Keith humbly, and then went on to pray a simple prayer of confession and to receive God's gift of his Spirit.

'Do you want me to tell your Mum?' asked David, when the prayers were over.

'Yes, please do,' responded the grateful inmate.

'I expect they will be pleased after all these years, don't you?' said the chaplain, grinning from ear to ear.

'Oh yes,' replied Keith, 'they'll be pleased. I'll tell my Mum myself tomorrow, I promise.'

Minutes later David was in his office, holding a neatly typed letter in one hand and a telephone in the other.

'Good morning, Mr Danes. This is David Powe, chaplain at Lewes Prison. I received your letter this morning.'

'Oh yes,' replied Mr Danes without much expectation in his voice. 'How nice of you to ring. I just wanted some advice really.'

'Well, I have some good news for you,' responded David.

'Really? Have you seen Keith?'

'Yes, I have seen him,' replied David, 'but it's more than that. He's come to faith.'

There was a long moment's silence at the other end of the phone before a further response, 'You mean he's become a Christian?'

'Oh yes,' said David, realizing there was more than a degree of surprise at the other end, 'you have been praying for him, after all.'

There was a flurry of activity as Mrs Danes was brought to the telephone, gasps of joy and amazement were expressed and the happy couple tried to assimilate this new information.

Two days later Mrs Danes rang David once more, 'We have to thank you,' she began enthusiastically. 'We came to see Keith, and when his sisters were at the drinks machine he told me. He told me he had become a Christian. It was all so easy. I can hardly believe it.'

David smiled at the receiver and asked that the family go on to help Keith in his new Christian life.

'Oh yes,' she replied, 'we know that, we must take it carefully, we have so much to plan, we really do.'

So Mr and Mrs Danes saw the answers to their long and earnest appeals to the highest court known to mankind. God had responded so generously, and witnessing that answer was a deep joy for us all, and a spur to faith for everyone who has heard about it since. We pray for Keith and his family, and trust God for his future, and we are also thankful that he has such a supportive family to whom he can return.

So that you can share in just a little of the family's joy at Keith's new beginning, there follow two letters we received regarding the experience from their point of view. They would wish others to be encouraged by their answer to prayer and to be an inspiration to relatives to go on bringing their loved ones before God. Although all the names have been changed in this testimony, the text of the letters has not been altered, and reveals how receiving a positive answer to a request can be quite a journey in itself!

Letter 1

Dear David,

Joe and I have experienced such a wide range of emotions since your phone call to tell us that Keith had become a Christian! The amount of prayer which has been dedicated to that young man by ourselves and others is significant! God **had** heard all our cries of longing ... but was this all too good to be true?

I suppose our feelings after the initial euphoria were, to be honest, of disbelief! You can read in books of wonderful answers to prayer in tragic circumstances but it couldn't really happen to our family, could it? And yet, you know deep down that our God is a wonder-working God and it **can** happen to us. We then said that we'd just wait and see what Keith would say, if anything! We weren't disappointed when we saw him on the Tuesday because, as I told you, he grasped the only few moments we were alone to say he had become a Christian. What an encouragement! However, the doubts still come to the surface. Does he **really** want to change or will life just carry on as before when he comes out? When you said Keith had been filled with the Holy Spirit what exactly did you mean by that? Has he had a very real supernatural experience he can hold on to, which even in the darkest moments he cannot deny? Please forgive me for voicing our feelings … my genuine prayer is, 'Lord I believe, help my unbelief!'

Perhaps a little of the background will show you how we have been very aware of God's fingerprints on so much of what has happened to Keith, and how his time in Lewes seems to be part of this.

Two years ago, while still at Art College, Keith was offered an unconditional place at a college to do an HND. He was very thrilled about this but over that summer of 1995, as he got more heavily into drugs, his interest waned, and by the time September came he had decided he didn't really want to start the course. We were bitterly disappointed because we felt he had been very fortunate to have been offered this place. However, as the beginning of the term came closer, he became a bit more positive and so I took him up at the beginning of October.

We had a horrendous summer with him and it seemed incredible that he had actually gone to College! As I drove home along the M40 I felt very thankful to God that we had reached this point. It was a very wet and stormy day and the sky overhead was dark and menacing. Suddenly the sun came out and in the spray from the numerous lorries on the road I saw thousands of tiny rainbows! A line from a hymn came into my mind ... 'I trace the rainbow through the rain' and I realized that the fact that Keith had started college at all was indeed a rainbow through what had been a very rough storm.

As the months progressed he subsequently got into more trouble, and the whole of 1996 was filled with anguish and heartache. But each day we endeavoured to trace a rainbow, to look for something positive to be thankful for, and when I found I was struggling to hold on to the Lord, he graciously pointed me to the very first line of that hymn, 'O love that will not let me go'.

One Sunday evening, shortly before Keith eventually came to court, the theme of our service was faith, based on the story of the healing of the centurion's servant. Joe and I found a lot of significance in the story. As we worshipped that evening, singing songs like 'Faithful One' and 'Great is Thy Faithfulness', I felt a real sense of joy ... not happiness because I certainly wasn't happy, it was joy, the same joy I had been surprised to feel at my

father's funeral … joy because you know your
faith is real and works in the darkest moments
of life. We finished the service with the hymn
… yes! … 'O love that will not let me go'.
When we reached the third verse, I sang with
conviction from the heart:

> O joy that seekest me through pain,
> I cannot close my heart to Thee,
> I trace the rainbow through the rain,
> And feel the promise is not vain,
> That morn shall tearless be.

When Keith was given a custodial sentence
in February 1997 and he was sent to Lewes,
numerous people said to us that God was
working in a wonderful way in Lewes Prison.
We knew that Keith would only be there for a
very short time, and Chris Lambrianou tried to
phone you and said that you were on holiday
for two weeks. Great! Just the very time that
Keith is there, the chaplain is on holiday, so
we thought! But in retrospect we can see how
perfect God's timing is. Keith had been in
Lewes for nearly two weeks, he had experienced the grimaces of life in prison, he had
been beaten up the night before and so must
have been at the lowest possible point, and you
came back from holiday and became Jesus' feet
and hands and brought his words of compassion and healing that Monday morning!

As I mentioned in my previous letter, the
first Saturday Keith was in prison I saw the

article about Lewes Prison in *Renewal* and I wrote to you to order a copy of the tape. The following week I saw a copy of the book, *The Cross Between Thieves* in our local bookshop and bought it. When I returned to the car I browsed through it while I waited for Joe. I was completely 'gobsmacked' (seems the only appropriate word!) when I noticed the title of the second chapter. 'I trace the rainbow through the rain' and saw the whole of my 'special' hymn written out in full. Wow! Lord! Your fingerprint again. I spent a large proportion of Saturday reading the book and what a thrill it was! Could it be possible that Keith could actually be impacted by what was happening in Lewes Prison?

You can perhaps imagine our feelings when you called on the Monday morning with the news! I came rushing down from our bedroom when I heard Joe's excitement! There couldn't really be anything else at that particular point which could have made him so ecstatic! I didn't need to ask him who it was, I think I knew but I couldn't really believe it!

We just need to exercise the faith and trust that, 'He who has begun this good work in Keith will carry it on to completion'. We'll continue to trace the rainbow through the rain because I'm sure there will be more storms ahead. However, we have come to realize that to be able to see a rainbow you need to be looking in the right direction! I'm sure that as long as we keep focusing on the Lord and his promises then we'll find 'That in Thy sunshine's blaze its day may brighter, fairer be'.

We still don't know how much longer Keith will be at Lewes and by now he may well have moved on (I recollect writing this once before!) but whatever the future holds we want to thank you for ministering to him at the very moment of his need.

With our love,
Mary and Joe

Letter 2 (one month later)

Dear David,

We had a phone call from Keith last night to say that he is in Dover. Initially Joe and I were disappointed he had moved on because Lewes has become quite special for us! We had started to think that perhaps he would stay there for his whole sentence. However, as we thought more and talked about it, we just felt an overwhelming sense of thankfulness that Keith had been able to stay at Lewes for as long as eight weeks!

In the six weeks since he became a Christian we have been hugely encouraged that Keith's trust in the Lord is genuinely developing. He is seeing the Lord's hand in specific situations … e.g. '… so there has been another miracle! I can't believe it!' The Bible has also been a source of strength and comfort to him, e.g. 'I read a bit of Psalms last night which kept my chin up a bit,' and then he wrote out the whole of Psalm 54 which obviously mirrored his own feelings at that particular moment. He frequently writes, 'I hope and pray that ...' and he told my mother in a letter, 'I have been to church for the past month, have a Bible and I read a Psalm every day which I find helps keep my strength and faith up.' He has also shown remorse when he wrote in a letter to Joe's aunt, 'I'm ashamed that you know that I'm in here and that you probably can't believe that one of your family is in prison. It is such a dark and chilling word, prison.' It is such a thrill to see the way that the Holy Spirit is opening his spiritual eyes. Forgive us for doubting ... the Lord is dispelling it!

Thank you again for all your concern and interest. We look forward to receiving your prayer letter in due course so that we can continue to pray for you all at Lewes. We trust that this is only the beginning of our links with you and that one day we might meet in person.

In a letter from Keith, which was written last Friday and arrived this morning, he says, 'I'll be going to church on Sunday. David is on holiday which is a shame because I wanted to say goodbye, but I can always write to him.' You have obviously meant a lot to him and perhaps you will get a letter one day.

The words which come into my mind as I wrote, come once again from that very special hymn, 'O love that will not let me go' ... from the last verse this time ...

O cross that liftest up my head,
I dare not ask to fly from Thee:
I lay in dust, life's glory dead,
And from the ground there blossoms red
Life that shall endless be.

Throughout this nightmare the Lord's powerful intervention has always been our source of hope and he has not let us down. Thank you for the enormous part you have played in helping Keith to discover that hope for himself. For Keith, life is beginning to blossom from the dust it had become!

    With our love and grateful thanks,
      Mary and Joe

Not all appeals to God are answered in the same way of course, and sometimes we grow to realize that the result we have so yearned for could lead only to disaster or at least disappointment if it were granted. Most of us fail to see that until much later, but Norman was one man who saw it early on, and whose response to God's seeming refusal should lead us to feel shame at our own feeble foot-stamping when our desires are thwarted.

Norman was in 'K' wing – the vulnerable prisoners unit – where he had been placed awaiting trial for alleged attacks on his own children. Norman hotly contested this accusation, and declared himself a victim of acrimonious false allegations. Only God knows the truth of men's hearts, but some men are indeed accused of false crimes from time to time, with horrendous consequences. Not being able to read minds, we had to take each man's word before God and leave the judgements to him.

Norman was devastated by his imprisonment, and was pleased to see David on his rounds. Norman responded instantly to the Gospel, although he had no background in Christianity and his father had even been an atheist. It was immediately obvious that the reality of Norman's faith was going to be a force for good, and although he couldn't join in Sunday chapel because of his 'K' wing location, he grew as a Christian at remarkable speed.

Most inmates in Lewes stayed only a few weeks or months at most, but Norman was to be there fairly long term, as his case was constantly subject to delay and requirements for further evidence. Quickly aware that Christianity meant changes, Norman set about altering his responses to other inmates. He began to be generous – an attribute virtually unknown on the average prison wing. When others requested coffee or other consumables, Norman would willingly supply them.

'What do I owe you?' the unsuspecting inmate would ask.

'Nothing,' Norman would reply. 'I'm a Christian. I'm meant to share.'

The astonished prisoner would shrug his shoulders and move on, probably thinking he'd found a soft touch. However, over the weeks the news got about, and Norman's amazing response to his possessions, in a world where so little means so much, began to gain respect. Norman had made his mark.

Naturally Norman prayed to God for his release. Feeling unjustifiably imprisoned must be a frightening experience and one in which it would be right to plead for help. Like Joseph in Genesis so many centuries before, Norman knew the pain of false accusation and loss of liberty inflicted by another's scheming. However, like Joseph too, Norman did not waste his time plotting revenge, complaining or blaming God. In fact, Norman's astonishing philosophy could put to shame most of our own responses to unfairness.

'I'm due for an end to my case,' Norman confided to David. 'I'm OK about that. I'd like to be out, but if I get twelve years, well, I'll take it that God wants me in here, doing my ministry.'

The ministry to which Norman referred was his general running of the wing, because in the nicest possible way Norman was the Christian baron of 'K' wing. Over the months the inmates had begun to trust Norman's impartiality and advice. He gradually took on the role of rota-maker, time-allocator and all round organizer of the wing's activities. The officers were pleased. With such a benevolent baron on the wing their job was rendered so much easier, as little escaped Norman's notice and everyone knew he was in control.

At one point three-quarters of the wing were Christians, and there were regular Bible studies in the coffee house – the extraordinary nickname for Norman's cell. When David went to visit him one day there were at least five interruptions.

'Will this tie do for court, Norman?' asked an inmate, anxious that he should look his best when up before the judge. Norman gave his advice and the man went out cheerfully.

'Ready for my reading lesson?' asked another inmate called Steve. 'Hang on, Steve,' replied Norman. 'I'm busy with the chaplain right now.'

Steve shrugged his shoulders and went out, knowing his reading lesson was coming. Steve was a short, thinly built man who could be described as inadequate in terms of education. He had responded to the Gospel in his straightforward way and was now being taught to read by means of Matthew's Gospel and Bible tapes. For me this was thrilling, as education in this country was originally initiated by a drive to allow the common man to read the Bible for himself. Although our education system has largely thrown out any links with making the Scriptures readily available to all, and even with any idea of real religious education, here was history repeating itself in a thoroughly rewarding way.

Steve was proud of his growing but still embryonic skills in learning, and was in no doubt that he was benefiting from being on the wing. 'I like it in here, David,' he told the chaplain. 'When I come back I'll do more Bible stories.'

David smiled inwardly. How could he tell this man that coming back was not a truly noble or appropriate aim for a new Christian – when to Steve it represented a stability of lifestyle he had never known, and a friend and mentor in Norman who surpassed any level of care he had ever experienced.

So David's visit to Norman continued to be punctuated by inmates' queries until it was time to move on to another wing.

'And all this,' David thought to himself as he left, 'without Norman even being able to go to chapel on Sunday or have but the barest structure of follow-up! God is indeed good and alive and leading men in Lewes Prison.'

One of the most humbling experiences for us in our dealings with Christian inmates was their inhibitions in responding to God. They were seldom hampered by inappropriate intellectual arguments about the possibility of divine intervention: if the Bible said something could happen, then it would happen; and if a member of the chaplaincy could pray in a certain way, then so could everyone else. The concept of hierarchy or special roles for ministers or people who were long-term Christians had no meaning on the wings of a prison.

A small group of Christian inmates were in a cell reading and praying when David popped in one morning.

'We're going to pray for Mike here,' said Tim, 'he's got this headache right across his head so we're asking God to get rid of it.' The inmate who'd spoken looked up at David confidently, and no glimmer of doubt crossed his face or echoed in his voice. He knew he was going to get a positive response. After all, why shouldn't he? Mike had gained his headache after a thorough going over he had received one night during a robbery. The pain just went on and on, and had not left him since.

Sure enough, Mike's headache left him and the men's faith and belief was strengthened, because Mike went all over the wing and communal areas declaring his release from pain and extolling the power of prayer! In the innocence and freshness of their faith, the men saw their prayers answered daily. Maybe greater tests of waiting and faith were in store for them over the years, but for now lots of them had no trouble at all in believing that God answers prayers.

We were being driven into even deeper realms of experience by all this, and almost daily occurrences of remarkable answers to prayer were a reality. For those who have the time to write and talk at length about the possibilities of prayer, there is always a satisfaction of the mind, but for those of us experiencing supernatural interventions as quite normal, there is also a sense of wonder, an inner affirmation of the power of God and a deep desire for others to witness the reality of that power.

Back on 'K' wing there was a problem Dan couldn't work out. 'These trainers keep moving,' he said earnestly but very straightforwardly to David.

'What do you mean?' asked David, who was used to having to drag details from inmates one by one, as filling in on minor, or often even the major, details never seemed to be an inmate's strong point.

'Well, they move across the room,' explained Dan, impatient that the chaplain didn't immediately grasp the drift of his meaning. 'At night,' he went on, 'they've definitely moved from here to here.' He pointed forcibly to each corner of the cell he shared with Joe. 'Joe saw it. He knows too,' he claimed.

David wasn't quite sure what was going on, but he had learned that strange things did occur and he was not going to disregard an inmates's concern, however bizarre it may have seemed.

'Well, it's odd,' added Norman, drifting into the cell, having heard that the chaplain was on his territory. 'This whole side of the wing has grown cold. The cells on that side are warm,' and he indicated across the narrow corridor that divided the cells, 'but this side is always cold.'

David now knew that something was up. 'Well, there have been some pretty evil things going on down here, Norman,' he explained. 'These things have their effects.'

Norman nodded wisely, and if he hadn't known previously about these occurrences he certainly wasn't thrown by the idea.

The previous week he had caught Steve with a ouija board, given to him by an unscrupulous and dubiously connected inmate who assured him it would help him find out what God wanted him to do. Not having been a Christian for very long, Steve had been none the wiser, although he was quickly put right by Norman once he found out. Norman was aware of the occult and its bad influence, although cold areas of the wing was a new concept, and he had not yet made any connection.

All the Christians on the wing prayed about the problem, and David brought Roy down, so that they could exorcise the area and ask God to fill the vacuum with his presence. The coldness disappeared, and there were no further reports of moving trainers.

The inmates took all this for granted of course, but David, Roy and I wondered at the way these events were now so commonplace and – well, almost ordinary. The prayers of the New Testament no longer seemed so distant from our own experience, and we simply had to exclude explaining away the stories of demons leaving and God's supernatural intervention in people's lives. It all served to make us bolder and more confident in our approach, both to evangelism and to witnessing and ministering outside the prison. Nevertheless, everything seemed very calm and relaxed, and there was no sense of whipped up emotions or unhealthy interests either.

Meanwhile we began to hear how God was answering our prayers for former inmates who had moved on or been released. Letters and Christmas cards began to arrive, not only from all over Britain, but also from all over the world, and we rejoiced that men were moving on.

Ken had been on remand, charged with a very serious offence, but had found Jesus Christ in Lewes Prison. A year later he sent us the following letter and poem which did encourage us as he intended, and which we hope will encourage many others who read it:

> Dear David, friend and brother in Jesus Christ,
>   Greetings!
>   I write this to you that it may encourage you and all, of the power and love of our LORD JESUS CHRIST, and to thank you, for it was on the 5th, this time last year, that you prayed over me, and JESUS forgave me, and touched my life, that it may never be the same again. I know that I have never felt so much love and peace as I do now, from that very moment,

there was a joy placed on my damaged heart, which came from life's cruel blows.

Since I was sent to this prison, and felt the reputation in which it does live up to, and all included, I have never seen such wonders to the glory of God in such a place as this. You see men come to Christ, to see them change their hearts, filled with hope, love for their fellow men, understanding and wisdom in words and deeds, is truly a joy to see. Only JESUS can change bad into good. As for me, every day is exciting, my spiritual life has grown, I cannot explain in words how the love of God has touched my life, all I can say is that he is my life, is with me always guiding me, comforting me and teaching me. The fellowships we have are a blessing, the friendship, a closeness is as if I have been given a new family where we help each other when difficult times come. Only good comes from God and forgiveness in love, Amen.

THANK YOU DAVID

Our fellowship has grown, and will continue to do so, for we were all lost souls until we asked JESUS into our lives and believed.

In this prison, all in fellowship with CHRIST join together in prayer at 11.00 p.m., we find there is much power in this form of prayer, which gives us all an opportunity to pray for revival and those in need, at 11.00 p.m. the prison starts to glow, because that's when they turn the lights off. Amen.

God has the perfect plan, and we are all part of that plan, which was given to us by his grace.

GOD BLESS YOU DAVID, in all you do and say,

Ken.

God wants us to plan.
but not to panic ...
To be busy
but not to be burdened ...
To be righteous
but not restless ...
To be working
but not worrying.
He wants us to have our minds on
what we're doing
while our hearts
are fixed on him.

How wonderful it was to receive such a letter and poem, and to witness this man's growth in faith in just one short year. Of course his path will be long and difficult, not only over the lengthy sentence that stretches before him, but also on his eventual release, but this man's hope shines through to us all and should urge us on to bring many more like him to faith. It is also helpful to know that Ken wrote to his victim in repentance and sorrow, and was reconciled to her in a remarkable way. God came into a life of appalling problems and redeemed it into something positive and good. The miracle of the power of the Gospel can be witnessed in this one man's response, and we are privileged to have seen it happen too.

John was now in Wandsworth serving his sentence, but he had become a Christian when David had been deputy chaplain at Belmarsh Prison, in London, prior to his move to Lewes. His letter is both moving and revealing as it indicates not only John's prayers but his concern for other inmates and David himself.

Dear David,

Greetings in Jesus' name. How are you, and how is fellowship in Lewes? I pray God is moving through his Holy Spirit and bringing more of the 'weak things of the world' to himself. Naturally, I mean the 'wanting' children of our world.

You asked me about using something I wrote in my last letter for some purpose (which escapes me). Well, yes of course, please do, if it will help in God's work. I'm too happy to offer a word or two.

I'm especially uplifted right now. Vineyard church visited me today. Well, the talk progressed and conversions were mentioned, particularly the hundreds at Lewes. At that time our C. of E. chaplain pointed at me, saying I had been converted 'at your hands' and was the 49th to be done so. I never forget you making a little note in your note book. From then on I knew I was going to be asked to share, so I did. It's the first time I have shared to any number of people that wonderful experience and the beginning of a life-changing process that is continuing daily – thank God. I'm very uplifted now and feeling so thankful to all he has and is doing. Relationships with my family are improving daily. God is so very good. I just want to keep recommitting myself to him. I recently had a dream that one of my sisters came to visit here. When I saw her I knew something wonderful had happened in her life, yes, she had given her life to Jesus. My heart leapt. It is very close to my heart. I pray it was a prophetic message and not just my emotion thinking. Carol, my youngest sister, has suffered for many years with internal ailments. And she has suffered when she wrote last time, she said that all she wanted was to be free from this constant pain. In and out of hospital she has gone and still the misery continues. I know Jesus can heal her, I know he wants to. If it is her that I dreamt about, I believe he will heal her when she decides to let him in. It only takes a committed 'yes' and that is enough. A family so torn over the years that is not only reconciled to one another but to God in unity as well is more than I could ask – but ask is what I'm doing!!

Over the years I have desired this more than anything. I had visions years ago of a reunited family. I felt that the 'buck' had to stop with me. Someone had to take the initiative or whatever, to change the situation. I didn't know how then. My own part in tearing relationships was very damaging. Fear and selfishness, pride and bitterness crippled me.

But now, a new creation, with the indwelling Holy Spirit and the kind of faith that could lead to all that God and I desire is happening. I am the first in the family to become a Christian. It is my responsibility to testify to them, to show them that God is as real and alive today as in the days when his Word was written. The Lord is pouring out his blessings on the nations, he is revealing himself in a way that cannot be denied. It is happening – today. I don't want my loved ones to miss out on the revelations of his promises.

I read a wonderful line from C.S. Lewis' *Mere Christianity* recently. He put Jesus' words of 'only believe' into another kind of image. Talking of food, he said, 'we don't know how food is nutritious for us, we know it is, but not how, we simply accept that it is'. If only people could accept Jesus as easily, instead of pussy-footing around saying things like, 'well, I'll just check the Bible and see if it says that,' or 'prove that he loves me'. I know it is hard to conceive for a lot of people, but 'seeing is not always believing'. More like, 'believing is seeing!!' I am almost preaching. Perhaps I should save it for those who need to know the truth.

It would be lovely to meet you again. The thought of it is exciting me already, ha ha. Well, David, I have another letter to write so I will close this one for now. I pray that you, your family and your ministry continues to thrive under the Holy Spirit's guidance, and the fruits of your labours are many.

Love in Christ,
John

I include these letters because they represent the many contacts we've maintained, and answer part of the question, 'Where are they now?' Many of our new Christians are still in gaol, spread over the country in various establishments. Some have found fellowship and help, others struggle to keep their faith. Only time will tell if their faith will stay the full course, even as it will tell if those of us from very different backgrounds will maintain the commitment too. Suffice it to say that they seem to have made a fairly sound start and appear to mean business with this new faith of theirs.

Some of the men of course are out and about by now, and one of our joys is to bump into them unawares. Dave turned up at the launch of my first book, *The Cross Between Thieves*, which our friends, Judy and Derrick, at Hunts' Bookshop had organized in Tunbridge Wells. Queuing up at the end of the evening, he was bursting to tell us that he had been supported by a local church and, by virtue of a series of amazing events, was able to set up his own second-hand shop called 'New Beginnings'. What a thrill to see him and hear him volunteer to come and tell others about his experiences! Here was a man breaking with the mould of his past and choosing a truly wonderful name for his new venture in trading.

At various churches we could see ex-inmates joining in the services, usually incredibly conspicuous because they always chose to sit at the front of the church as in chapel, and were blissfully unaware that many established Christians come early to service just to sit at the back!

Outside McDonald's we bumped into Roger, who beamed from ear to ear. 'I'm glad I came to Lewes,' he blustered. 'I've put my life right. I came to chapel every week and went to carpentry class. I go to college now to learn more carpentry.' Then as he turned to go away, having thanked David profusely for his help, he added, 'I still go to church – the local Methodist, you know.'

'Well done,' we responded in unison as he walked off cheerfully, obviously pleased to have met us once more, although this time in happier circumstances.

Paul was in the local car park working as an attendant when he acknowledged that he knew us. David wished him well before he was ushered forward by the car behind. One glimpse was all we had, but we could see from his smile that Paul was a happier man.

So too was Ryan, who literally ran across a road in Brighton as we were heading towards a theatre to see the Victoria Wood show.

'Can't stop,' he blurted out, 'but thanks for all you did. I'll never forget you.' With that he was gone, but the brief encounter lifted us more than any theatre visit could ever do.

So from time to time we are sent full and encouraging news from ex-inmates, and at other times we are only granted the shortest meeting, but we receive sufficient feedback to inspire us onwards, and we are well aware that for many people work and prayers are given without any knowledge of results at all. We are fortunate and blessed and we know it.

Of course some people are desperate to test the ministry by finding inmates who would 'prove' or 'disprove' the case, and some seem to believe that inmates should show a rate of growth that would be exceptional or even unique inside most churches. This kind of evidence is not granted, and in terms of most ministry we know our prison one can only be said to be in its infancy. Most people take years to develop deep Christian faith, although of course a sizeable number do sprout significantly, and we know our Christians are likely, for the most part, to experience the same somewhat bumpy ride.

We aren't surprised, therefore, when we meet some of our 'men' once more inside the prison walls, for having, as they put it, 'slipped up, Gov'. Most are terribly shamed faced and full of excuses and apologies, but nearly all go on to recommit themselves and re-establish their Christian lives. Of course this happens in all Christian ministries, so why not in prison, too? Nevertheless, it is a sadness when an inmate returns and has to be helped back on the path. It is always taken seriously, but pleasingly the occurrence is remarkably rare.

All these fellows are the subject of much prayer and we shall never know how the appeals to that higher court, made by so many members of our prayer line and interested churches, are the stimulus or cause of the burgeoning faith of so many new Christians. We thank God for the faithfulness of the pray-ers, who seldom know the results of their pleadings but who take it on themselves to lift prisoners and ex-criminals to the heavenly court in order that they might finish the race they have chosen to start when they first find faith in prison.

✳

CHAPTER 8

How Much Do You Think You're Worth, Boy?

Is a rich man worth more than a poor man,
A stranger worth more than a friend?
Is a baby worth more than an old man,
Your beginning worth more than your end?

Is a president worth more than his assassin.
Does your value decrease with your crime?
Like when Christ took the place of Barabbas,
Would you say he was wasting his time?

Well how much do you think you are worth, boy?
Will anyone stand up and say?
Would you say that a man is worth nothing
Until someone is willing to pay?

I suppose you think that you matter,
Well how much do you matter to whom?
It's much easier at night when with friends and
    bright lights
Than much later alone in your room.

Would you say they'd miss one in a million
When you finish this old human race?

Does it really make much of a difference
When your friends have forgotten your face?

Well how much do you think you are worth, boy?
Will anyone stand up and say?
Would you say that a man is worth nothing
Until someone is willing to pay?

If you heard that your life had been valued,
That a price had been paid on the nail,
Would you ask what was traded,
How much and who paid it
Who was he and what was his name?

If you heard that his name was called Jesus
Would you say that the price was too dear?
Held to the cross, not by nails but by love,
It was you broke his heart, not the spear.
Would you say you are worth what it cost him?
You say no – but the price stays the same.

If it don't make you cry –
Laugh it off – pass him by,
But just remember the day when you throw it away
That he paid what he thought you were worth.

How much do you think you are worth, boy?
Will anyone stand up and say?
Tell me what you are willing to give him
In return for the price that he paid?

'I don't care what you've been told,' said Terry Tully, the visiting speaker, 'you're not worthless.' There was already an air of concentration in the chapel, because the inmates appreciated Terry's ministry. A builder by trade, he had suffered greatly in his personal life, not least by the premature and unexpected death of his son. His immense sorrow over this tragedy was kept in balance by his very real and personal faith.

'If Jesus can't help me through this, then what's it all about?' he said to David and me.

He certainly had the gift of communicating his message to the prisoners, and they knew that his comments were genuine and powerful. Terry went on, 'When I was at school I was hopeless. I couldn't add up and my writing was bad. I was told I was rubbish and I'd never make anything of myself.' He looked round at the assembled men. 'I guess some of you know that feeling. But let me tell you – one day I met someone who told me about Jesus and that God loved me, and my life changed. You're not worthless. Don't let anyone ever say that to you again. God made you and he thinks you're valuable, whatever anyone else may say!'

The men were thinking. You could see from their faces that many were identifying themselves with this man's testimony.

'You're rubbish, no good, worthless', would all have been words used about them, and many would have heard such abuse so often as to be unable to consider themselves in any other way. Low esteem, in spite of displays of amazing bravado, was the norm. Most people outside have suffered from varying degrees of lack of confidence, in spite of having no real grounds for it, but some of the prisoners have experienced year upon year of abuse, failure and rejection. Being of value or worth to themselves or anybody else is quite often a meaningless concept, and certainly feelings of inadequacy are emphasized by being caught up in the judicial system.

When accused defendants stand before the magistrate or judge and jury at the culmination of weeks or months of preparation, they know they will hear the verdict of society upon their lives. In others' hands lie the decisions that will affect their futures. Their autonomy is gone and they can only hope for fate or clemency to deal them an acceptable hand. They tend to know all about court procedure, even if they have not attended one before, because many other men have and information is easy to get. Everyone's life is open and discussed, because for men who have to live, eat, sleep and even attend to basic bodily functions in public, there is little reason to hide the common experiences of a trial.

Consequently the men all know about the strengths and weaknesses of various judges, courtrooms and briefs, and what has happened to every other inmate whose time comes up for the reckoning. Tuning in to local radio is an essential skill, or someone's crime may be secret and their fate unknown. Knowing about everyone else is an almost universal interest, and is naturally immensely satisfying – until of course your turn comes up. Then all the feelings of inadequacy, rejection and uncertainty rear their ugly heads for your own case, and the perception tends to make a 'subtle' change. Now the spotlight of interest fixes on you, and it makes for very uncomfortable emotions of both vulnerability and loneliness.

I can remember a period of my life when I was very vulnerable and feeling alone. I had moved to college – Gypsy Hill College, Kingston – for teacher training. Unlike the apparent mass of students who were thrilled with the freedom of it all, the communal independence was not for me. I was after the qualification and wanted above all to teach, and this endless round of coffee cups, lectures and preparation was personally unsatisfying. I was also removed from my cosy world of church social life and support, and my lack of independence probably shocked me most of all.

Several things kept me going. The first was Mondays, as they were main subject study days. I was very fortunate to be taking Biblical Studies as my main subject – a course only available at Gypsy Hill, which consequently drew many evangelical Christians to study there. I was incredibly influenced by Peter Cousins, Old Testament lecturer and later an editor of Paternoster Press, who opened my eyes to the Old Testament and thrilled me week by week by being simply the most stimulating lecturer I have ever heard. He had an amazing ability to take a sometimes narrow evangelical viewpoint, reveal its flaws in terms of intellectual criticism, and then give really satisfactory answers to questions that many of us had refused to face. Thus serious open-minded Bible criticism became an enlightenment, not a faith-destroying activity.

I shall never forget him for illuminating the Old Testament in that way.

Anne Long was our New Testament lecturer, and she was responsible for the second positive experience at college. (Later she went on to Nottingham and then to be involved in the Acorn Healing Trust.) Anne instigated a dance drama group called Charis, about which she later wrote a book called *Praise Him in the Dance*, and in this group we interpreted the miracles and parables of Jesus' life through the medium of dance drama. Although this experience was in its infancy in terms of being shared by the Church, the members of the group grew immensely in their understanding of the power of the gospel stories, and I shall also never forget the influence of that group on my life.

The third major sustaining factor at college was far more mundane – it was the possession of a cassette recorder. As I write now it is a cause of real amusement that owning such an item could have held such significance, but it certainly did. I had never previously possessed anything like it and I was fascinated by it. My cousin owned one and I can remember being really jealous, hardly imagining that one day I would have one myself. I managed to be frugal in the first term and bought the cassette player proudly one Saturday just before Christmas. I also purchased a simply hideous lime-green canvas bag in which to store and carry this fairly substantial item, and took it back to my tiny room in the digs.

I opened it all up with great care, and although I had no real tapes to play, I took my single blank

C60 and practised playing my guitar and singing into a mike propped up on a copy of Bright's *History of Israel*. What a thrill to play it back – I was truly delighted. However, I was to be more excited still as I began to acquire various tapes to play on my own in my room. One holiday I discovered Graham Kendrick's 'Paid On The Nail' recording, and simply wore it out as I listened again and again to this talented man, who in the 1970s was plainly light years ahead of other contemporary Christian artistes.

Various tracks on this and other tapes were to be hugely important to my Christian life, not least of which was 'In Your Way And In Your Time', basically a prayer of submission to God, that his ways and times are certainly not usually what we expect but nevertheless always the best. I never forgot that song, and sang it with a friend at various weddings and Christian events all down the years, always finding that it would touch each listener with its deceptively simple words and flowing melody. However, it was another track that I was to recall more than twenty years later, when one morning we visited an Icthus church in London and spoke to Graham Kendrick himself about his forthcoming first visit to Lewes.

'Please sing that song, Graham,' I requested quietly, 'the one called "Paid On The Nail". It is so relevant to our men.'

So it was that Graham began to use that song in our services, to extraordinary effect.

'It's as if it were written for prisons like this,' I joked with Graham one morning.

'Yes,' he replied with a broad smile, 'it is, isn't it?'

The song was so powerful in the prison context because it utilized this very concept of worthlessness. Yes, I had felt inadequate and without real value in that college setting, but compared to our inmates I know nothing of feeling unappreciated. Nobody ever shouted at me that I am rubbish, and I have never been totally bereft and overwhelmed by a feeling that no one, literally no one, cared about me. Plenty of prisoners, and come to that probably other members of society, have heard such abuse and felt such utter rejection. To men such as these the words of Graham's song rang a great many bells indeed.

How much do you think you are worth, boy …
Would you say that a man is worth nothing
Until someone is willing to pay?

Whenever Graham sang all eyes were fixed, all ears trained on the words.

'Held to the cross, not by nails but by love', continued the song – beginning to offer the hope that someone did indeed care for each individual in that chapel.

Then the song moves to its climax. If Jesus loved me so much as to die to pay the price for me, then what is my response?

If it don't make you cry –
Laugh it off, pass him by –
But just remember the day when you throw it away
That he paid what he thought you were worth.

The music rose with each line of this challenge, and as it quietened down again everyone was trying to grasp the meaning that Jesus paid what he thought we were all worth when he died – and he deserves a response for so doing. Graham had used this powerful song in the chapel several times before we took him to the vulnerable prisoners of 'K' wing. 'K' wing reminds you of scenes from films where prisoners are interrogated by evil guards and acts of appalling brutality are carried out. Of course the treatment of prisoners is more than fair in Lewes, and life bears no resemblance at all to the films. Nevertheless it must be the low ceilings, lack of real daylight, and sense of being underground that cause the comparisons in my mind, and whenever I step up and out into the daylight of the prison courtyard I can only feel a huge sense of relief that freedom is a reality for the majority of us.

A small group of inmates gathered on chairs, not knowing what to expect, looked up at this stranger. There was nowhere to plug in the guitar, no mike, no music stand and certainly no plans. Graham began to play various songs and received sincere applause after each one. One man in the front row sat seriously consuming his packet of Doritos one by one, before finally screwing up the packet loudly and stuffing it into his pocket. Several got up and left and then returned later. Two radios were playing in the background, and a group of men were a bit grumpy because the pool table was out of use during this impromptu event, and it was their association time being used up. At the end of the wing, two officers stood in the office or 'bubble' looking down at the scene, and behind them the air conditioning unit buzzed regularly, as men trooped in and out of the toilet and wash unit.

Halfway through an alarm bell went off in the wing above, and all the red alert lights down the wing began to flash on and off, much like the blue lights on top of speeding police cars.

The majority of Graham's audience, however, ignored all these seemingly disconcerting events, and listened attentively to this man who had bothered to come and play to them. Obviously it must have been unusual for Graham to say the least, but it didn't show in his ministry. He began to play 'How much do you think you are worth, boy?', and it became obvious that the acoustics were on his side. Everyone was concentrating, moved and inspired, not least David and I, and it was also evident that the singer was totally absorbed and filled with the Spirit of God.

Afterwards this generally rejected group of men shook hands with Graham one by one and thanked him sincerely for his appearance.

'You could take this up professionally, you know?' suggested one inmate helpfully. 'Right,' replied Graham with a smile.

All the ministry at Lewes is working towards the aim of telling inmates that they do have a real value and are in truth worth a great deal in the eyes of God. All the evidence of their lives might work against it, but the gospel message of a new purpose is true. We want as many men as possible to face their earthly judgements in court upheld with the certain knowledge that Jesus is with them. If they know about all the traumas and vulnerability of standing in court, either from past experiences or from other inmates, we wish them also to know that they have a real person in Jesus to stand beside them too.

The idea that Jesus is their advocate and friend is an easy concept to grasp. They all have briefs and people who plead for them in court, but they all also know the inadequacies of the system. They need and want someone to answer up for them, and the concept that Jesus might just be the one has strong appeal. What is harder to grasp is the knowledge that this special person, Jesus, actually took their place when it came to facing up to God's judgement. After all, who'd take the rap for anyone else unless forced to?

David told them one morning about Barabbas.

'Now there was an evil man,' he explained. 'He was due to be executed for his crimes and he was banged up, probably in the segregation unit, with no hope of reprieve. Suddenly two screws burst in the door, "Barabbas," they cried, "on your feet!" '

Everyone in chapel that Sunday sat forward. They were all interested.

' "What now?" thought Barabbas,' David continued. ' "Am I being shipped out, even ghosted?" ' (This term refers to moving prisoners without prior warning to either inmates or relatives, and represents a generally disliked practice.)

The congregation of inmates smiled and nudged each other as the story moved on.

' "No," Barabbas was told, "you're free. Get out now." The prisoner looked bewildered, "What do you mean?" he asked.

' "This Jesus, Jesus of Nazareth, will be taking your place. He has done nothing wrong – but he's going to die. I shouldn't ask questions, just go." So Barabbas left, probably thinking Jesus was crackers, but free all the same. Jesus took Barabbas' place, but he did more than that,' David explained, as everyone tried to take it all in. 'He took the place of everyone – me and you and he will give you a fresh start if you want one this morning. You'll be free like Barabbas – not to go on with your old ways, but rather to find new ways of life – this time with Jesus at your side.' David went on to ask if there was anyone who would like to come to him afterwards and find Jesus for himself. That morning five people responded in faith, because of course Barabbas' story is a very powerful one and God certainly used it on that and many other occasions.

In chapel that morning was Kenny Jones, a really committed Christian whose faith story was told in *The Cross Between Thieves*. After Lewes he had gone to another prison and then on to release. Unfortunately he had been involved in an incident concerning various dubious items and was back in on remand. Although this incident was a far cry from his previous convictions for appalling violence in his pre-Christian days, and he assured us he was not really guilty anyway, he knew he should not be inside at all.

'Sorry, David,' he offered, the first time he saw David on the wing. 'I have kept my faith, you know. It is hard, but I have. My wife's gone and I have custody of one son. It's been tough but God will sort me out I know. I'm going on with Jesus.'

Whatever the ins and outs of his reappearance at Lewes, there was no doubt that this slight, wiry, previously highly dangerous man, with his gappy grin, was 'going on'. Within one week his cell mate Danny came to faith and was off his heroin habit. Within two weeks he was leading a whole group of inmates up to chapel, virtually in a line, to 'come and hear David'; and within three weeks he had organized a Bible study of twelve men, nicknamed the dirty dozen, so that Roy would come and teach them all about the Bible.

'You have to give it to people straight,' he explained to David. 'No mucking about. They'd better come up and find out what God's about if they don't know. So I'll bring them.'

In chapel there was Kenny in the front singing 'Majesty' as loud as ever, and raising his fist in a salute every time Jesus' name was mentioned. One visitor remarked it was strange we were all so pleased to see him again, but we just couldn't help it. He was such an inspiration.

This time the Reverend Stephen Nunn picked him up and welcomed him into his parish in Hastings, and helped him thoroughly through his bail period. Kenny was to join Howard and lots of other ex-inmates in that church, which was a shining example of Christianity in action, prepared to take those whom so many others would not. Indeed Howard became a member of the Parish Council Committee, voted in against opposition from another candidate. We were sure he would have very valuable insights to offer that no one else would be able to share in quite the same way!

Kenny's story, however, brings us to a very important point. Instant middle-class conformity and value systems are far from the grasp of lots of prisoners. If we set targets which exceed the bounds of reasonableness, they will fail miserably, and possibly give up. We do see inmates again as they battle against years of habit and overwhelming temptations, but it doesn't mean they are no longer in the faith. I'm not tempted to steal, so I can't really pride myself in not doing so. I am tempted, however, to be very impatient, and will often fall to that 'crime'. Do I then castigate myself and believe my faith is no longer valid? Of course not. I perceive it as a falling down, a slip up, a regrettable occurrence. Many of my failings will never be known to others, and I won't face public recrimination for them either, but in God's eyes they are just as bad, as Jesus made clear when he said hate was of the same nature as murder and lust a degree of adultery in God's sight.

Similarly, although we want our new Christians to grow and expand in their faith, we have to be realists, not only about their lifestyles but also about their ability to fit into the average church grouping. Time after time we meet ex-inmates who have become Christians in prison and who are now out and about. Always they greet us, always they shake our hands, and thank David for his prayers, and always they have the light of God's love in their eyes.

Those who work in prisons know that generally the eyes of inmates are sad or bad or downcast at least. The change in the eyes of those who meet with God is quite remarkable. A sparkle, a glimmer, call it what you will, is present, often right from those first precious moments of new life. This light in the eyes continues and is in evidence whenever we met ex-inmates.

Maybe we notice it in them especially because of the dullness or lifelessness that held sway there once before, but whatever the cause, you just can't miss the power of that witness.

In C.S. Lewis' mighty children's story *The Lion, The Witch and The Wardrobe*, the children ask the professor how they will know if other people have been to Narnia – the magic land that represents the essence of Christian experience to so many readers. The answer is that there will be something about the eyes of someone who has been there and experienced meeting Aslan the Lion – the Jesus figure from the book.

For us this has been the case too, and as we've bumped into those often young men while going about our business, they have that certain something about their eyes. Often they have not linked up with a church, although some have, and we want to encourage them to do so. But we have had to learn to let them go, as Jesus obviously did in the gospel stories, not knowing where they were ending up but trusting their lives to the Father God who drew them to himself in the first place.

Now some Christians may be dismayed by this, finding it inconceivable that anyone could go on with God without being a fully-paid-up card-carrying member of a local Christian group. But we all need to broaden this view, offering help and encouragment to all who are open to faith if we wish to reach some of the outer edges of society with the Gospel. You cannot apply the same rules to a highly educated, middle-class, articulate and socially acceptable convert as you can to the average prison inmate. Their interests are poles apart, their skills and abilities totally diverse, and their needs as different as chalk and cheese. The challenge for all of us is to find ways of opening our churches to such people without forcing them into our preset mould. We must focus on the true elements of spirituality and help them to grow in those, rather than demand that they interest themselves in certain limited activities. Of course some churches are brilliant at welcoming, supporting and nurturing converted prisoners, but while they are few and far between, we can hardly be surprised if substantial numbers of inmates cannot take the pressure of some fellowships and have to plough a rather lonely furrow. Obviously this is not a desirable state of affairs, but it is still a reality for many. The surprising and indeed joyful thing for us is to see men still glowing and trying to put things right in their lives, in spite of little or no support, and the crucial thing is to pray for a greater understanding and willingness to help on the part of church groups everywhere.

Sitting at the back, way behind Kenny during the service on Barabbas, was Paul. He knew all about feeling worthless because he had experienced weeks and weeks of regret and remorse when he first came into the prison. One day he had completely lost his temper at a gathering and attacked a man with whom he had disagreed. Grabbing the first thing that came to hand, a large and substantial saucepan, he had used it to settle his grievance in an uncharacteristic but very violent manner. His poor victim suffered real damage to his head and was hospitalized immediately. A full recovery was unlikely and Paul found himself under arrest for grievous bodily harm. David met him early on entry and offered him God's amazing offer of forgiveness and a new start, but Paul would have none of it.

'I'm not worthy,' he wailed, leaning over his knees and obviously grief stricken. 'I can't forget it. I don't know why I did this. No one can ever forgive me.'

Later in court Paul displayed considerable grief in front of the judge, confessing his crime openly and with shame. He was placed in the hospital wing because he was suffering from debilitating stress, and eventually, but very slowly, he began to accept the love of God, even for him, by regularly coming to chapel. One day he took up God's offer of new life and became a Christian, and the effect was almost instant. Still smitten by his deed, he now knew he was forgiven, and his shining eyes were seen every week in the chapel, as he joined in the service fully and with joy. God had eventually spoken to Paul's heart and convinced him that he was not worthless after all. We doubt he will be in trouble again, although of course he will have to live with the effects of his crime for the rest of his life.

Jake was another inmate in that chapel scene who was struggling with the concept of worthiness.

A young offender, he met David on the wing and had a chat with him in his cell.

'I'm not up to much,' he said, 'I can't even get my life right either.'

'Why's that?' questioned David.

'My mother is a witch,' declared Jake, a very straightforward and unimaginative lad, 'she's put a curse on me and I'm not sure why.'

'She might have done just that,' assured David, 'but God can remove it, I promise you.'

Jake indicated both surprise and interest. 'Really?' he asked.

'Yes,' replied David calmly.

Bowed in prayer, Jake became a Christian, and David denounced the curse placed upon him. It was all quite calm and meaningful, and afterwards Jake looked very relieved. The next day Jake told his mother on the phone that he was now a Christian, and she was not a happy woman. There followed a stream of abuse; calls to David's office and threats of revenge were to follow. Jake, however, went on in faith, and became a strong Christian on the wing. His feelings of worthlessness were dissipated, and he had found a new sense of value in his relationship with God.

As we work with the men we realize there are no real barriers to being welcomed into God's family and finding worth there, apart from those to which people wished to cling. Everyone's need is different and results from any one of a huge number of causes, but Jesus, the only real friend and advocate of all, is able to give new purpose and relief to all who seek Him.

This is true, of course, in every walk of life, not only in prison, but is probably more obvious there, because of all the sad and difficult backgrounds. Just as he did on earth, Jesus is giving value to these rejected members of society and is declaring them worthy. Many find that their new friend is with them when they go for their cases to be heard, and face the consequences of their actions, and many too will have the further and much greater thrill of seeing Jesus by their side when the time comes for them to face that final and ultimate judgement at the end of their lives. Every reader of this book needs to be sure that they find their value in terms of their relationship with Jesus too, because it is the only value or worth that will count in the end. It is easier for those of us outside prison to perceive our worth in terms of our job, power, education, money or human relationships. Valuable and attractive as all these things are, they will count for little when God assesses the state of our life's work and experience. He will wish to know how we stood in relationship to his Son and we will stand or fall by that alone.

Yet it would seem that it is the prisoners who have a truer picture of their position before God, and realize their need of a saviour more readily than others. This could seem an unacceptable message for many, who will feel grossly superior to people who are banged up in a prison. Nevertheless the gospel message is that everyone has fallen short of God's glory and needs the forgiveness and acceptance of Jesus to be able to reach God. The question, 'How much do you think you are worth?' is one for us all to answer honestly, and is a clear reason for us all to make sure we are in a sound relationship with God himself.

CHAPTER 9

✳

The Ultimate Court Appearance

All prisoners have one momentous advantage over those of us who have never been part of the penal system, namely that of experience. Inmates comprehend the emotions involved in passing through the hands of the judiciary, and the frustrations and consequences of failing to convince a jury of their innocence.

It is neither fashionable nor 'spiritually correct' today to talk about religion in terms of judgement. One could be justified in believing that the wheel of Christian understanding has turned a full 180 degrees from its position in other ages, and now concerns itself only with aspects of God's nature that refer to his all-embracing love and forgiveness. Any sense of being called to account for one's deeds is seldom, if ever, the subject of serious consideration.

The truth would appear to be that the theology of God's universality of embracing love is interpreted to require any concept of guilt to be quashed as unaffirming or exclusive, and any perception of duty to the lost to be regarded as at best slightly misguided and at worst positively embarrassing. One can imagine that a glance at the Bibles of some Christians would reveal scores of passages removed or crossed out, especially in relation to some of Jesus' own sayings regarding facing God and the final judgement.

Inmates in our prisons seldom develop such sensitivities to the idea of being answerable for their deeds. The vast majority of them do not complain about the legitimacy of the court trying them, as their attention usually centres on either pleading their innocence or on emphasizing mitigating circumstances. They know that their chances are spent and that they can no longer run away. Facing the music, or rather the judge, is all that is left, and the feelings are not comforting.

One Sunday the 'story' in the chapel was centring on God's call to each man to face up to himself.

'When you come to the real court after you die,' David was explaining simply and seriously, 'you will have to face God and the books he opens. In these books will be all the things you've ever done and all the things you haven't done. You will be judged by these things.' David looked around the room and could see he had everyone's attention, with every eye upon him. After a short pause he continued, 'You'll be on your own then. No brief will plead for you or explain your circumstances, and there will be no co-defendant there to either support you or take the blame. God knows all about you. You won't be able to hide at all. He won't let people get away with things.'

The mood was serious but not heavy, and everyone was following the argument with no difficulty.

'But there is another book called the book of life, and if your name's in there, then you won't be judged at all. It's Jesus' book – the one that holds all the names of the people who've asked him to take over their lives. Let's look at the Bible together!'

David told everyone to open their Bibles at Revelation 20:11–15. As usual this took some time, and various volunteers helped some inmates find the appropriate page. Sensibly and with a great deal of effort on behalf of some, the passage was read aloud,

> Then I saw a great white throne and him who was seated on it. Earth and sky fled from his presence, and there was no place for them. And I saw the dead, great and small, standing before the throne, the books were opened. Another book was opened, which is the book of life. The dead were judged according to what they had done as recorded in the books. The sea gave up the dead that were in it, and death and Hades gave up the dead that were in them, and each person was judged according to what he had done. Then death and Hades were thrown into the lake of fire. The lake of fire is the second death. If anyone's name was not found written in the book of life, he was thrown into the lake of fire.

After the congregation had finished reading there was a short pause and then David added, 'Jesus was grassed up, you know. He died even though he'd done nothing wrong at all. The truth is he took the rap for you and me.' He pointed round the room ending with himself. 'Everyone who wants a new start this morning can have one because of what he did. If you'd like to go to heaven when you die and have a new life right now too – then you'll need your name to be in Jesus' book of life! Come and see me afterwards if you'd like that.'

The closing part of the service took place quietly, and afterwards men began lining up for tea and jaffa cakes as usual.

Dick, a young man from the back, remained still. David approached quietly and sat beside him. 'OK?' he questioned.

'I'd like my name in there,' said the pensive inmate, 'in that book of life you were talking about. Does it mean even me?'

'Oh yes,' replied David, 'it certainly does.'

Several others that morning found faith in the Good News that Jesus could help us to find God, but no response was more rewarding than that of Dick's.

He was not the only inmate to have responded to this passage, and although of course it is only used from time to time, there is no doubt that the Holy Spirit uses it to bring people to Jesus. One can almost see the brains of the inmates ticking over, and several reported just what they had been thinking: 'Fancy my experience being in this book. How did they know how I'd feel? These books of life sound just like I've seen in court. Those briefs seem to have all the answers about what I've done and

I guess God knows it all too – though I've never thought about it before. Judgement at the end – that sounds awful. I know what it'll be like. I really do. I'd better do something about it right now.'

Now some people seem to think that the only legitimate approach to Christianity is made by someone who has carefully weighed up the pros and cons, probably attended a course, and has made a decision in cold, emotion-free circumstances, fully aware of all the implications for the rest of a lifetime. To them the sheer rationality of God's love must drive the decision, and any swift and therefore 'dubious' response to God should be the subject of the greatest suspicion.

In reality people respond to God for an infinite number of reasons, just as they did in the times of the Bible, and just as they have done ever since. Who, after all, can put their hand on their heart and say that their relationship with God started and indeed continue with only the purest and most cerebral of motives? Or perhaps go further and even question whether cerebral motives are the only ones that count anyway?

Some people gradually move into Christian things even from childhood. They never seem to struggle to find faith, but rather it all comes as a natural progression. Some meet God in periods of fear, either of life's situations or of death, and others face God when crises of various kinds raise their heads. Some seek out of inquisitiveness or a feeling of helplessness, and still more find God out of boredom or a sense of pointlessness. The reasoned, rational approach to finding God must find its place amongst all these other responses, for it would seem that God uses the whole gamut of human experience and feeling to bring people to himself. If the result is real and lasting faith, then who are we to question the route through which another approaches Christianity? One thing is sure: that we meet representatives of all these groups in prison. In spite of their variance of approach and a propensity of those who come through a realization of a final calling to account, they all have one thing in common – the Holy Spirit himself calls them. For no man will respond to an argument or an appeal to take on faith, however effective they may be, unless God works in his life to show him the truth of the message.

When the followers were out and about in the first century, spreading – or as the original Greek says, 'gossiping' – the Gospel of Jesus, there were those who envied their power over demons and illness. Simon the sorcerer was one of these, and he approached the Christians in an attempt to acquire or buy the power. He saw the reality of the Good News of Jesus and the power of God, but failed to tap into the experience because he was coming via the wrong route. God's power and love are freely given but only to those who seek God in honesty and faith.

Jerry was down on the wing when there were a large group of Christians seeing remarkable answers to prayer.

'I want some of that,' he said to a Christian inmate, 'I want that power,' but of course it was not for the inmates to grant access to the power of God in that way, and the man attracted only by the results of faith was not able to respond to the need to find faith in his own heart.

So those who felt that the team were in some way frightening inmates into the Gospel were missing the point. Firstly, no one came to faith whom God had not touched, and secondly, telling people the truth about their own status before God can hardly be called putting unnecessary fear into people if it's true. No, God was using the inmates' present condition and circumstances to bring them to himself, and those of us who've met the resulting Christians are in no doubt that their response is totally valid.

The problem for many of us outside is, however, that we find it hard to come to terms with final judgement. If we really believe in it surely our sense of urgency for spreading the Gospel will be immense. Somehow we manage to live Christian lives, often steeped in Bible verses or having participated in hour after hour of Christian worship sessions, without grasping the reality of the inevitability of judgement. While on earth we may escape many of the experiences described in this book. We may manage to live by law-abiding principles, either out of fear or of genuine belief in their value, and thereby steer clear of the police, prison and the whole court experience. We may even fail to feel the slightest empathy with those who do undergo the rigours of the law, feeling that they receive only that which they richly deserve.

Nevertheless, one day we will all surely be in their shoes, see the view from where they stand,

public disgrace

and share with them the ignominy of being found out and being called to account for our deeds. At the end of time we will all face the ultimate court experience and the judge will be God himself. Now of course this is picture language, but perhaps the images we acquire from the worldly courtroom are helpful in giving us a 'feel' for the event and a glimpse of the seriousness of the issue. The Bible plainly teaches us that everyone has both done wrong things and failed to do good things. Although we are all often able to escape the results of our sins in this life, this will not always be so.

God has given us life and the world in which to live, and he expects us to live a moral and good life in response. Everyone fails to do so, and the result is that we are cut off from God's love, and will find there is a barrier between him and us when we come to face him at the end of our lives. Everything will then be known, there will be no secrets and no place to hide. We will all have to hear God's verdict on our lives, and unfortunately for every man and woman the result will be the same: 'Guilty' will ring in our ears. There will be no special pleading, no cries of 'He's worse than I am', or allowances for circumstances, because, in some way or other, we have all fallen short of the ideal.

There is of course one huge relief in this horrific scenario, and that is that for some the judgement will not be a fear. Those who have chosen to accept Jesus into their lives and serve him on this earth, instead of themselves, will find that all their guilt and responsibility has been placed on him – the only sinless man the world has ever known. He takes the rap – our place in the dock and our separation from God – and we go free into a new life with him. Amazing? – yes. Too simple? – no – just God's plan to bring us back to himself. No wonder the first Christians called it the Gospel or Good News of Jesus!

So perhaps we can find a tiny patch of room to envy these inmates in our prisons because they understand the seriousness of their condition. The final court may not be such a surprise to them, only to us, who believe in our own good standing. We suffer from an illusion of superiority at our peril, only a true comprehension of our state before God will help us to see what we must do.

Lee knew what he'd done was wrong, and at the end of a service had a fair idea of where he stood before God. A slight, short figure, he looked very young indeed to be inside, although the truth was that he had murdered someone during a fight, and was so high on drugs and alcohol that he had no recall of the events that led him to face such a serious crime.

As the final prayer finished he literally ran to the front and knelt down by the platform. His short blond hair was all that you could see from the back, but he looked up at David with large doleful eyes and pleaded, 'Can God forgive me?' Later he went to the hospital wing and informed the volunteer that, 'My Mummy knows I'm here.'

Lee's life was a total mess by anyone's standards, but he found God that morning, because no problem is too great for the one who made us all. It is a matter of attitude of heart and a willingness to start again that counts.

In contrast to Lee's slight frame, Des was a heavy-set, big bloke who had short hair and tanned skin. He was imprisoned for GBH because he had thrown someone in front of a passing car during a fight. Although on drugs like Lee, he was luckier, because the man he assaulted had not been killed.

Des had asked to see David, but the officers were on their toes that morning and were being protective.

'Not in there, David,' said one officer firmly, 'he's dangerous, that bloke.'

'Well, he has asked to see me,' replied David, anxious to find out what Des needed.

'Well, we'll come with you,' said the officer, obviously concerned for David's safety. 'All three of us,' he continued, beckoning to two fellow officers in the 'bubble' on the wing.

So the four men approached Des' cell, and David spoke through the hatch. 'Des, do you want to see a chaplain?'

The man inside leapt to his feet. 'Yes please,' he replied.

The officer opened the door and the three colleagues watched as David stood in the entrance – these situations were always tricky, and anything involving the safety of the chaplain was important. What happened next was a huge surprise and rather uncommon. The large inmate immediately threw himself at the chaplain's feet, and vast hands gripped David's ankles firmly. Uncontrollable sobbing rose from this obviously penitent man as he cried, 'Can God help me?'

Before responding to this needy inmate, David turned to the somewhat astonished officers and said, 'I think I'll be all right with this one after all, but thanks all the same.'

The officers realized that they could leave, and with a few raised eyebrows left David to it.

Oblivious to the officers' entrance or exit, Des continued to grasp David's ankles in sheer desperation, and although the story has its amusing side it is clear that Des understood his need of God in a way that many others never do. He found faith that day in that cell, and went on to be a real disciple. His problems did not fall away, but he had a new start and a brand new companion in Jesus. His pride certainly hadn't kept him from finding a faith that's sure.

By contrast, Mark had thought about Christian commitment for years and years. A young, bright man, he was posted on the segregation unit nevertheless, because he had had some bother on the wing. His fairly cheerful, if very spotty face confronted David one day and pronounced, 'I've thought about this for years. Lots of my friends and family are Christians and they've prayed for me for ages. Guess I'd like to join them now.'

The apparent ease of this transfer from one side of the fence of belief to the other belies the effect of prayer for him offered by the wealth of Christian contacts he was so privileged to enjoy. Nevertheless his step of faith was real; he had made the move himself, and the jolt of prison could well have been the deciding factor. Quite a contrast to Lee and Des but with the same result – a new Christian beginning his own individual path of faith.

A further example illustrates the range of approach for those who seek to get right with God. During a service, as usual David and the rest of the volunteers prayed for wisdom to know just who needed help that day. Having prayed with two other men, David glimpsed Paul going out of the door back to his cell. The chaplain sprinted the few yards down the chapel, grabbed Paul's arm, and asked, 'You want to accept Jesus this morning, don't you?'

Paul stopped abruptly, and the officer in charge helpfully waved him back into the chapel. Tall and good looking, Paul was dressed all in black, so David knew this was a man on remand as he was not wearing prison clothes. Paul sat for a while with David and, like so many before, gave his life back to God in simple prayer.

Afterwards he looked gratefully at David and said, 'Thank you for finding me out this morning. I really wanted to come forward but I didn't quite make it.'

'That's OK,' replied David, 'you made it in the end, that's all that counts.'

Indeed that is what counts and it illustrates once more how many need to be asked personally to respond to God, because in spite of a real desire to find him, they lack that confidence to ask for help. It is for us, the Christians, to offer that assistance, and if we fail, who knows how many miss a real chance of new life?

David began to end the talks he gives to outside churches with a vivid picture of the end of our lives, because we have grown to be immensely concerned that an urgency for the Gospel be rekindled.

Although it is true that the actual judgement concerning life or death will pass Christians by, because the decisions they make on earth give them the right relationship with God to enter heaven, nevertheless they will be called to account for the stewardship of their time and talents.

'Just imagine,' David would say, 'you go to meet Jesus and he asks, "What have you done with your life?" You will reply, "I attended the church in Wentby for sixty years. I ran the youth group, sat on committees and was their best worship leader ever."

' "Good," Jesus will reply, "I know this; did you learn anything on the way?"

' "Oh yes – I read my Bible daily and studied notes and commentaries all the time. I toyed with New Testament Greek and led many a Bible study."

' "All this is good," Jesus will reply. "So you knew all about me for sixty years?" You will nod your head in muted pride of course, but perhaps then he will ask pointedly, "Did you bring anyone with you?" '

At this point in most meetings there is a deep silence, as everyone begins to take in this questioning of their own response to the commission of Jesus to tell people about him. It will, of course, be a very sad day if at the end of our lives we have failed to bring anyone with us. The spread of Christianity was surely the result of a huge chain reaction, as each new convert passed on the Good News. In the first century the Gospel spread as people moved about the then known world. They took huge risks to bring the Gospel to foreign shores, and eventually even to our own. The life of the Church depends on us all taking up our part in the telling of others, and yet somehow we can escape this task by reassuring ourselves that we are not all evangelists.

Of course we don't all have the same gifts, and there will always be those who excel in this area, but it is for all of us to be witnesses to the Gospel of Jesus. If we leave it all to the few, the Church will fail in its mission. Direct evangelism may be out of vogue, and it is easy to join the bandwagon of laid-back friendship-style programmes, but quite often Christians can be so laid-back about evangelism that they appear almost horizontal in their approach. Naturally our friends should be attracted to God through our lives and faith, but does that really mean that only those with the benefit of a Christian friend can hope to hear God's message of hope to the world? I trust not; indeed, if we truly want to take seriously Jesus' command to spread the Good News to others we will have radically to reappraise our own attitudes to the society in which we live. If we really still believe that everyone will have to face God's judgement one day, then we are at best irresponsible and at worst highly negligent if we fail to tell them now.

The truth does seem to be, however, that we are just a little embarrassed about the concept of final judgement, and would perhaps prefer it to be a little less severe than the Bible writers warn us it will be. However, before we eliminate ideas of judgement from our Christian vocabulary, on the grounds that a loving God will let everyone off in the end, let us check the basis for our decision, because it is doubtful that either Scripture or Christian tradition will provide such evidence. In terms of history, it is only recently that Christians have fought shy of declaring God's judgement on the world and on the individual. Could this be because we now lack the drive of the persecution of ages past, or because we just have an overwhelming desire to be both liked and perceived as very reasonable and rational? Whatever the grounds for our reluctance to accept a concept of judgement, I would challenge the position as wishful thinking. I believe the reality is that we will indeed face judgement at the end of our lives, and that this truth should drive us to spread the news of Jesus to everyone we can.

I also believe we should all be motivated to hear God's 'Well done' in preference to a truly awful awareness that we personally brought no one with us.

One of our chaplaincy team was Stan, a faithful but now retired Salvation Army Officer, who was an immense support to the ministry at Lewes. He had spent a life's work passing on the Good News of Jesus whilst also helping people in many practical ways. Taken to writing poetry, he shared the following poem with us one day, and we feel it to be highly significant to our own ministry, and an inspiration to others to find places where they too can share the good news.

PRISON VISITING

Thoughts on Matthew 25:36, 39, 40

'I needed clothes and you clothed me, I was
sick and you looked after me, I was in prison
and you came to visit me.' 'When did we see
you sick or in prison and go to visit you?' The
King will reply, 'I tell you the truth, whatever
you did for one of the least of these brothers of
mine, you did it for me.'

'I was inside and you visited me.'
Visited you, Lord, how can that be?

I visited lonely and broken men
And sought to renew them in hope again;
I went to the call of a youngish bloke,
And sat and talked while he had a smoke;
I spoke to a man just divorced by his wife
Because he is serving a sentence for 'life';
I entered a cell that was dark and grim
To a man who was reaping the wages of sin;
I went to a cell full of hatred and tension,
And your precious name, I hardly dared
    mention.

And yet, Lord, you say I was visiting you.
I find it quite hard to believe that is true.

'Inasmuch as you did it unto the least –
Of these labelled "scum" and "vicious beast" –

Yes, even these here, the worst of men
I am pleased to call my brethren;
It was even for these that I bore sin's pain
To bring them right back to my Father again;
And though it is hidden and hard to see,
In each one of these there is something of me;
So bring them my love and help them to see
That I died to make them totally free;
I rose that they too my life might share,
And eternal reward begin even in here.'

Dear Lord, in my visiting this is my prayer
That with every man this Good News I might
  share;
That though he may feel he is loved by no other,
Jesus is pleased to call him 'My BROTHER';
And Lord, in each cell, this is my plea:
Each man may see something of Jesus in me!!

Stan Ozanne

This wonderful poem contains the essence of the Good News about which we have been talking throughout this book. Jesus died to set everyone free whatever their past may have been, and to give them an eternal life that begins here and now. God himself yearns to relieve us all from hearing that ultimate verdict of 'guilty' ringing in our ears. He sent his Son to bear that verdict for us in ways that, although beyond our comprehension, are totally valid none the less. His love reaches out to us all to give free consciences and a new start in life. If you have never found that love and release yourself, then maybe today is the day of decision and discovery. Be assured he will not reject you, but has indeed great plans for you in this life and a warm welcome once the time comes to meet him face to face. Hundreds of prisoners have joined the many thousands outside gaol in finding the gospel message to be as true today as it was two thousand years ago. Many of them have been driven by a crisis to see their need, but it is not necessary to have shared their experience of crime in order to find a new life.

At the end of this chapter there follows a simple prayer such as many, many people have prayed down the centuries when they have meant truly to seek God for the first time. The actual words are not important; rather, the desire of mind and heart indicate that something very special is taking place.

The paradox is made clear – those who lose their lives by surrendering to God, discover that they may actually find them in tremendously exciting service to him.

There are countless witnesses to vouch for the trustworthiness of God, and those who pray such a prayer discover themselves part of a vast body of believing people. Of course it takes honesty and real courage to change one's life – many other belief systems seem to make so little moral demand in comparison – but God has made the cross of Christ the point of decision for us all, and his final verdict on us will depend on the responses we have made to his precious Son. As for Jesus, he has clearly promised that those who confess to him in this life will find him by their side both now and in the next life too. It is on this basis that the Christian Gospel is proclaimed throughout the world, to the men and women of this country, and that includes the inmates of any prison.

I trust that the stories in this book have inspired you to see how God is working today in bringing people to him. I also hope it is an encouragement to play a full part in evangelism with renewed commitment and enthusiasm. There is a tendency to demand greater proof of a dramatic kind before we accept former criminals as Christians. Many church members, who may fail to exhibit such sustained and substantial evidence of their own growth in faith, may still require an inmate's conversion to transform him instantly if his first steps of faith are to be accepted. Those of us privileged to work with them, however, rejoice at their sometimes tentative moves towards God, are frequently amazed at the strength of their conversion, and are prepared to wait for God himself to issue his final verdict – on both them and us.

*
Prayer of Response

Father God,
   I realize that your final verdict on me would be that I have both done wrong things and left good things undone. I am truly sorry, and earnestly wish to change my ways. I ask Jesus to take over my life so that I can live a new life now, and live with you in heaven when I die.
   Fill me with your Holy Spirit so that I may have the power to make changes in my understanding and behaviour.
   Thank you for loving me in Jesus' name. Amen.

If you have prayed this prayer with sincerity and honesty, then God has accepted you whatever you may feel. Do tell a Christian friend or minister of your decision, for they will be able to help you further.

Every Blessing,
Gillian and David Powe

The Reverend David and Mrs Powe can be contacted at:

Chaplaincy Dept
HMP Belmarsh
Western Way
Thamesmead
London
SE28